THE
BRIDESMAID'S
DAUGHTER

THE BRIDESMAID'S DAUGHTER

❖

From Grace Kelly's Wedding to a
Women's Shelter—Searching for the Truth
About My Mother

❖

NYNA GILES
and Eve Claxton

St. Martin's Press
New York

www.stmartins.com

Designed by Kathryn Parise

Grateful acknowledgment is made for permission to
reprint lyrics from "California Dreamin'."
Copyright © Hal Leonard LLC.

THE LIBRARY OF CONGRESS CATALOGING-IN-PUBLICATION DATA
IS AVAILABLE UPON REQUEST.

ISBN 978-1-250-11549-2 (hardcover)
ISBN 978-1-250-11551-5 (ebook)

Our books may be purchased in bulk for promotional, educational, or business use.
Please contact your local bookseller or the Macmillan Corporate and Premium
Sales Department at 1-800-221-7945, extension 5442, or by email at
MacmillanSpecialMarkets@macmillan.com.

First Edition: March 2018

10 9 8 7 6 5 4 3 2 1

To my mother, Carolyn,
whose beauty and kindness are forever
imprinted on my heart.

And to anyone suffering in silence,
in the hope that you may find your voice.

PROLOGUE

The day my mother's story first slipped out into the world, I was twenty-nine years old. It was March 1989, and I'd just dropped my daughter at her nursery school before driving over to my local A&P supermarket to pick up groceries. My son was still a toddler, sitting in the shopping cart, kicking his little legs as he waited for me to pay at the checkout. I remember glancing down and smiling at him as I stood on the line. He was such a sunny and easy child; I looked forward to our time alone in the mornings together after his big sister went to school and before his midday nap.

My husband and I lived with our two young children in a nice, comfortable house in a suburb of New York, the same town that he'd grown up in. I was a stay-at-home mom; I spent my days taking my children to playgroups and nursery school, to their doctor's appointments and the supermarket. Our friends were my husband's college friends and their wives, people who knew almost nothing about my family or my past. I preferred it that way. I thought I could keep everything neatly in its place, the same way I cleared up the children's toys before my husband came home at the end of the day.

That day at the supermarket, the woman ahead of me in the checkout was still unloading her groceries from the cart, so I turned to glance at the magazines in the rack as I waited. And that's when I saw it. The headline on the cover of one of the tabloids.

PRINCESS GRACE BRIDESMAID LIVING
IN N.Y. SHELTER FOR HOMELESS:
PHOTO EXCLUSIVE

I whipped around to make sure no one else had noticed. My face was on fire, my stomach tight.

No one in my world knew about my mother, about the connection to Grace. Would they even guess that the woman from the headline had anything to do with me? I grabbed a copy from the rack, tucking it under a quart of milk. Then, as fast as I could, I paid for the magazine and the groceries and fled to the parking lot, unloading the shopping bags and little Michael into the car, before climbing into the driver's seat and slamming the door behind me.

In the quiet of the car, I opened the magazine, searching for my mother.

There she was, on page nineteen. Gray circles under the hollows of her dark eyes and streaks of silver running through her cropped black hair. In the photograph, she was sitting on the steps outside the shelter where she lived, wearing a thick white scarf around her neck, pausing to place a small knitted hat on her head. For the most part, the article about her was accurate. My mother *did* sleep each night in a homeless shelter on the Upper East Side of New York. Her bed was number eighty-five, a small metal cot covered with a regulation blue blanket, in an open dorm. Each morning at 7:00 A.M., the guards shook her awake, and she got up and left the shelter, going to Bergdorf Goodman's department store to wash in the basins of the ladies' lounge, spending her days in the local parks, libraries, and churches.

The part about Princess Grace was also true. My mother and Grace Kelly had first met in New York in 1947 when they were teenagers living in next-door rooms at the Barbizon Hotel for Women. Grace was studying acting; my mother was modeling for Eileen Ford, and had just arrived in New York from Ohio. After Grace became famous, the two women remained close, and when Grace married Prince Rainier in Monaco in 1956, my mother had been at her side as one of her bridesmaids.

The article went on to explain that since Grace's death, Carolyn's story had taken a very different turn. Now, only a few years after Grace's fatal car accident, Carolyn was "lonely and destitute," living in a shelter.

What the article didn't say was that while my mother may have been lonely, she was *not* alone. She had family who cared about her, who tried to persuade her to seek help, to find housing. Each month, I accepted her collect calls, and my husband and I paid a local diner so she could eat her meals there. I was the bridesmaid's daughter, and while I might not have told my friends and acquaintances about her situation, I thought about my mother all the time. I worried about her, hoped that she was warm enough, leapt every time the phone rang, terrified something had happened to her.

And as often as I could, I went into the city to visit her. My mother and I would meet in a little square set between buildings on West Fifty-eighth Street where she liked to sit and pray. She was religious, devoted to the Virgin Mary, and she believed the little square was blessed. I knew I could always find her there, sitting on a bench, her head bowed, her hands clasped in prayer. From a distance, no one would have guessed my mother was homeless. Not a hair on her head was ever out of place. Proper appearance was always very important to her. She liked to wear white for purity: white slacks, white shirt, white scarf, white tennis shoes.

Together, we'd go to a nearby diner for lunch, spending the next hour or so picking at our food and trying to make conversation.

My mother usually wanted to talk about astrology. She was obsessed with star signs and the movement of the planets.

"The planets are colliding this week," she'd say, shaking her head. "We have to be very careful. It's a dangerous time."

She was always concerned, always anxious. She had a lot of advice. If I talked about my husband, she'd tell me I should leave him. If I brought up something about my children, she told me that I should take them to the doctor; she was worried about their health. She was concerned about me, too. She wanted me to see a doctor; I didn't look well.

"We need a miracle," she'd say to me. "I've been praying for a miracle for you."

But when I tried to talk to my mother about what we could do to improve her own situation—how we could help her find a stable place to stay—she'd shut me down.

"We'll talk about it when the sun is shining," she'd say.

And that was that. She didn't want my help. More than anything, she seemed to want to be left alone. I had spent so long trying to separate myself from my mother, forging my own life in order to survive; I'd even changed the name she had given me, Nina, spelling it with a *y*, to set myself apart. Now, as we sat on the opposite sides of the table at the diner, it was as if a thousand miles stretched between us. During those lunches, we were careful to avoid eye contact. My mother looked off to either side, remaining alert to danger. I stared at my plate. I didn't want to catch my mother's eye; if I did, I usually regretted it. She had the saddest eyes I'd ever seen.

After lunch, I got back in the car and drove home to the suburbs, back to the careful, normal life I had built for myself, my fortress.

My mother remained living at the shelter for a decade, until 1998. At that point, she developed a heart problem, which meant she could no longer legally stay at the shelter, and we were able to move her to an adult home on Long Island. She spent her last years at a nursing care center, where she died in 2007 at the age of seventy-nine.

When my mother was alive, I never managed to learn what had made her the way she was, why she was so removed from the world, how the once glamorous model and bridesmaid ended up sleeping each night in a shelter. It was only after she was gone that I was finally able to understand what had happened, to go back to the past, in search of the woman my mother had been before I was born— and to the childhood I'd lost after everything changed.

Part One

BEFORE

CHAPTER 1

Carolyn

The young woman in the photograph isn't my mother yet, and she isn't Grace's bridesmaid. It's the summer of 1947, and she's still Carolyn Schaffner, about to leave Steubenville, Ohio, for New York City. She's so young, barely nineteen years old, slender and pale-complexioned, with angled cheekbones and her dark hair in a pageboy, smiling out at the future ahead of her.

Carolyn had wanted to live in New York for as long as she could remember. Growing up in the little clapboard house on Pennsylvania Avenue in her hardscrabble hometown, she always felt as if she belonged someplace else, if she could only figure out how to get there. Her parents had divorced when she was young, her father moving away to Virginia. Her mother, Dorothy, was dark-haired like Carolyn, with the good looks of a movie star, and she quickly remarried. Dorothy had two more children with her new husband, Joe. Carolyn often felt that her half brother and half sister were her mother's real family, and that she—Carolyn—was somehow on the outside, watching them from a distance. Joe ran a small laundry service. Carolyn's new stepfather was a tall, coldhearted man, who believed that her role in the house was to provide unpaid labor for the benefit of him and his children. There were always dishes for her to clean, messes to clear up, her brother and sister's clothing to wash. The smog of Steubenville's steel mills left behind a layer of grit on every surface of the house that, despite her weekly scrubbing with pine and Lysol, never stayed away. It was easy to displease Joe. If Carolyn missed her curfew in the evening by as much as a minute, her stepfather would bolt the doors and refuse to let her in. Then she would have to stay with her friend who lived across the street, or walk three miles to her cousins' house to find a bed for the night. When Carolyn returned in the morning, the stack of dishes in the kitchen sink was still there from the night before, waiting for her to wash them.

When Carolyn was younger, her birth father, Harold Schaffner, would occasionally come to visit. Each time, Dorothy would warn Carolyn, "the bad man is coming." Before long, the visits from the bad man stopped and it was only when Carolyn turned fifteen that she decided she wanted to seek out her true father. She went to the local police chief and asked for help. The police chief managed to track down Harold in West Virginia. That summer, Carolyn spent two months with her father, meeting her two half siblings there.

After she graduated from high school, she got a job in the local department store, in the children's shoe division. She worked and saved as much as she could, but she worried that if she stayed in Steubenville too long, she'd end up marrying a local boy, and then she'd never escape. There were so few options for a young woman in search of an exit, but Carolyn had an important asset. Ever since childhood people had complimented her on her appearance: her dark brown eyes, her winning, natural smile; her blue-black hair that lay sleek to her head. While she was still in high school, a teacher introduced her to a commercial photographer, who offered to take some test shots. Carolyn started reading every fashion magazine she could lay her hands on, studying the models, their expressions and poses, practicing at home in the mirror in her bedroom.

The summer after leaving high school, she saw her opportunity. Steubenville was celebrating the 150th anniversary of its founding— its sesquicentennial. As part of the celebration, the prettiest girl in town would be crowned Queen of Steubenville. First prize was either a trip to Hollywood for a screen test or five hundred dollars. Carolyn entered the contest and campaigned for her votes, knock-

ing on doors and enlisting promises of support. She won, none of the other girls coming close to her beauty. As queen, she presided over all the sesquicentennial activities, riding in the parade on the biggest float of them all with the words HER MAJESTY emblazoned on the side. Carolyn waved from her silvered throne as the people crowding either side of the street cheered for her. For four nights, she appeared in a historical pageant staged at the local stadium, playing the "Queen of the Festival" in front of an audience of thousands. Her photograph—wearing her blue and gold cape and jeweled crown—was front page in the local newspaper. People recognized her as she walked down the street.

When it came time to choose her prize, Carolyn turned down the ticket to Hollywood; she wasn't interested in acting. Instead, she took the cash prize, using some of it to pay for a one-way ticket to New York City. Carolyn wasn't going to follow the pattern set by Steubenville, or by anyone else's expectations.

In New York, she would try her luck as a model.

A girlfriend drove her to the Steubenville train station to catch her train. Dorothy had to stay home and make dinner for Joe and the children that evening; she couldn't leave them, even to say good-bye to her own daughter. So when Carolyn left, there was no one from her family to see her off. As the station platform and her hometown disappeared into the distance, it was almost as if she'd never been there at all.

Thinking about the day, I wonder how she got up the courage to do it. How did a young, single woman in 1947 find it within herself to leave her family and move to another city without any idea of what came next? How unhappy must her life have been at home with her stepfather on Pennsylvania Avenue that she felt so motivated to escape?

Perhaps my mother believed that staying in Steubenville would require a different kind of courage, one that she knew she couldn't muster.

A DAY LATER, Carolyn stepped down from her train at Penn Station, and caught a cab to 140 East Sixty-third Street. She read all the fashionable magazines, so she knew that the Barbizon Hotel for Women was the best place for a girl to stay while in the big city. Barbizon residents were models, actresses, singers, students, and secretaries, girls who, like Carolyn, wanted to make something of themselves. The hotel's rooms were reasonably priced, and most important, as male guests weren't allowed much farther than the lobby, she would be safe.

Most of the hotel's guests, not only the out-of-towners like Carolyn, would have been intimidated at first sight of the Barbizon. From the sidewalk, even if you craned your neck, it could be hard to see the tip of the building, twenty-three stories high, with dark brown brick terraces and setbacks, like a giant, somber wedding cake. Carolyn pushed inside the revolving doors and into the lobby, nearly as wide and as deep as the building, with a curved staircase sweeping up to an ornate wooden mezzanine. Nervously, she walked toward the front desk, where a small, smiling woman was waiting to greet her. This was Mrs. Sibley, the hotel's manager. Carolyn handed over her references while Mrs. Sibley looked her up and down.

Candidates for residence at the Barbizon were assessed on their references, as well as their age, looks, and background. The management's preference was for attractive girls in their late teens or very early twenties—and with a waiting list of at least one hundred names, Mrs. Sibley could have her pick. At nineteen, Carolyn met the age requirement. As for her pedigree, Mrs. Sibley most likely assumed that Steubenville was a steel town and that Carolyn's parents were solidly blue-collar. Fortunately, Carolyn was pretty enough to pass Mrs. Sibley's test.

Then Mrs. Sibley read Carolyn the hotel rules and regulations. No cooking appliances in the rooms, lest the building burn to the ground. No liquor in the rooms. It was the hotel's preference that young ladies did not stay out late at night but returned to their rooms at a respectable hour. A warning would be given to anyone who didn't comply. If, after a warning, the girl continued to stay out late, Mrs. Sibley would have to inform management, who might decide to give her room to another girl. As a guest of the hotel, Carolyn had the use of its swimming pool, gym, library, and roof garden. In the afternoons, complimentary tea and cookies were served in the recital room, on the mezzanine above the lobby. Should she wish to join, backgammon and card games were held in the evenings in the recreation room, and there were regular educational lectures on a range of subjects, to improve the mind.

But Mrs. Sibley and her fellow staff of the Barbizon weren't only seeking to improve the minds of the young ladies of the hotel. They were also determined to protect their virtue. No men were admitted beyond the lobby, Mrs. Sibley warned Carolyn, unless a guest wanted to bring her date to the coed lounge on the nineteenth floor, in which case a special pass was required. And after sundown, male elevator operators were switched for female ones, in case any man should be tempted beyond his station.

CAROLYN'S ROOM WAS on the ninth floor, and like all the Barbizon's rooms, it was tiny and narrow; you could almost stretch out your arms and touch the walls on either side. There was just enough room for a small single bed with a nightstand, a desk with a radio, and a table lamp. The green drapes matched the bedspread and the carpet. Bathrooms were shared and situated at the end of the hall. Carolyn didn't mind. From her window, she could look out across the rooftops of the tan-colored town houses of Sixty-third Street and beyond to the entire city. Even after midnight, she learned, the streets were alive with noises: traffic, taxi horns, and the voices of people passing down below. For twelve dollars a week, this world was hers.

At the Barbizon, Carolyn did her calculations. She had nearly two thousand dollars in her pocketbook, made up of her prize winnings and her savings. This was more money than she had ever possessed, but still, she wasn't naïve. She knew it wouldn't last forever. She thought about signing up for a modeling school but feared the cost. In her room, she kept her folder of test shots, taken back home in Steubenville. She had posed down at the golf course, wearing the dirndl skirt she'd made herself in black and white stripes, her dark hair like satin and her lips painted and full.

Each morning, Carolyn dressed as if preparing to go to work, pulling at the fingers on her gloves until they were perfectly straight, pinning her hat on her head at the ideal angle, then taking the elevator down to the lobby. There she stood and watched as the hotel's residents hurried out of elevators, chattering to one another as they pulled on their gloves and adjusted their hats, before streaming through the revolving doors, out into the world and their lives. More than anything, Carolyn wanted to follow them.

And so she did. Mostly, she walked, saving the subway or cab fare and learning the city as she went. She discovered Bloomingdale's department store, right around the corner from the hotel, where she could admire the latest fashions. Walking farther, she stumbled on the Horn & Hardart Automat, just south and west of the hotel on Fifty-seventh Street. The food at the Automat was cheap and fresh, and stored in little glass boxes. You dropped the nickels in the slot, turned the dial, and then popped open the door to pull out your selection. Carolyn thought the Automat was so modern and clever, as if you'd just stepped into the future. No one minded if she stayed for hours, sitting by the window upstairs, looking out onto the hats of people passing by on the avenue below, only getting up to refill her cup of coffee from the spout in the wall. In Steubenville, when she went home at the end of the day, she spent her time clearing up after her younger siblings, washing dishes, cleaning house. But after she ate at the Automat there were no dishes to wash. And when she went back to the hotel, her room was her own; it was cleaned, and the bed made and turned down. She was free.

One day, only a week after she arrived in New York, Carolyn was at her usual spot at the Automat, looking out over Fifty-seventh, when a young man came up to her. He introduced himself as a photographer.

"You're an attractive girl," the young man said. "Ever thought about modeling?"

Carolyn told him yes, and that she'd even had some test shots taken while still home in Steubenville. The young man sat down; they started talking. The photographer knew people. He could introduce her.

Would she like to meet Harry Conover, owner of one of the oldest and largest modeling agencies in the country?

Carolyn nodded yes. The young man scrawled an address and number on a piece of paper—52 Vanderbilt Avenue. That day, Carolyn left the Automat and ran back to the Barbizon with the paper in her pocket, the ticket to her new beginning.

CHAPTER 2

Nina

That young and determined woman at the Barbizon is a person I never knew. By the time I was born, my mother was in her early thirties, married and living on Long Island, spending her days taking care of my two older sisters and me. When I picture her back then, I see her standing at the stove in our kitchen, head tilted slightly. She's wearing her everyday blouse and slacks, either in white or pale pink. One hand is stirring something on the stove; the other is holding on to the counter. To one side is a glass of wine. Her cigarette is in an ashtray, and when she picks it up, she twirls it in her fingers absentmindedly. My mother is quiet and methodical in her movements as she stirs. Classical music plays on the turquoise turntable she keeps in the kitchen. I'm standing behind her, quiet as I can be, always worried she might startle if I make too much noise.

In my earliest memory of my mother, I'm still a baby. I've just learned to walk, and I've somehow maneuvered myself over the bar of my crib, sliding down onto the floor below, then going out along the hallway to the stairs overlooking our living area. I turn around to shuffle down the stairs on my knees, going about halfway down before I call to her. My mother's standing below at the kitchen counter with her back to me. When she hears me call, she runs to me, scooping me up into her arms, protecting me. Even as a baby, I'm searching for her, trying to keep her close.

When I was growing up, my mother and I were often in the house alone. My father was almost always someplace else, either working or socializing in the city. My two sisters were six and eight years older than me; they had their own lives, their friends and places to go. Our house was at the end of a long private road, surrounded by woods, at the edge of the waters of Long Island Sound. My father called our home the Dream House, and he had helped to design it. The Dream House was built from planks of redwood trees, with ceilings two and a half stories high. At the back of the house were giant picture windows from floor to ceiling looking out over our own little beach, where I liked to play. The house was very modern, ahead of its time, but at night, when the wind was blowing, the Dream House creaked and complained, as if it never wanted to be built at all.

Through the woods and up the hill was a castle called Eastfair. This was the home of my father's closest friend, Sherman Fairchild. Sherman was a millionaire and he had built the castle for himself, modeling it on a medieval French château he had visited while traveling in Normandy. The castle was vast and made of stone, with a tall tower at one end, of the kind in which princesses are imprisoned in fairy tales. The Eastfair estate had twenty acres of grounds, indoor and outdoor tennis courts, a pool, and a big square building with a photography studio inside, where Sherman would take pictures of the models that came to visit him on the weekends. It was Sherman who had given us the strip of land on which to build our home, and Sherman who threw the parties my father attended while my mother stayed at home with me.

When my older sisters, Jill and Robin, were home, I did my best to keep up with them. I took note of what they wore, what they said, how they acted. I wanted to have what they had and to be a part of whatever they were doing. This came with its risks. I remember standing and watching my sisters playing with the tree swing that my father had rigged up in the woods to the side of our house. I knew I was too young to join in, so I stood to one side. The swing seat was made of wood and metal. Jill climbed into the tree, and Robin was pushing the swing as high as she could so that Jill could grab it and leap on.

"Nina!" Robin shouted, warning me to get out of the way.

I turned just as the metal swing hit me right on the top of my head. My sisters carried me back into the house, leaving a trail of blood all the way across the gravel driveway, up the steps, and into the kitchen, where my frantic mother tried to stop the blood with towels. When it became clear that the cut was severe, they took me to the emergency room. I remember how frightened I was, the feeling of being restrained, my arms strapped into a papoose, aware of every stitch the doctors sewed up my head.

Later that evening my father came home to find a bloody driveway and what looked like a murder scene in the kitchen. He had no idea where we were.

IN MY MEMORIES of my mother, she's almost always at a distance, turning away from me, lost in the daily tasks of motherhood. I don't think she particularly enjoyed cooking, but she did it diligently, moving around the kitchen slowly and methodically, completing each task by rote. Her dinner staples were hamburgers (always without a roll) and baked potatoes and peas. Sometimes she'd heat up Tree Tavern Pizza, or make chicken or shrimp curry with white rice, or filet of sole with butter sauce. My favorite was her breakfast: one egg over easy on white toast with crumbled bacon and salt and pepper, all chopped up together. She'd bring it to me in bed when I was sick. Once in a while, she'd make me a special treat: chocolate chip pancakes arranged in the shape of Mickey Mouse's head—a circle for the face, and two smaller circles for the ears. She smoked all the time as she cooked, finishing one and lighting another. Newport was her brand; with its turquoise-and-white packaging, and the gold paper lining, it seemed so much more feminine than my father's Kents.

When she wasn't cooking or driving my sisters to their various activities, my mother was doing laundry. The laundry room was upstairs next to my parents' bedroom, and it had a washer, a dryer, an iron and ironing board, and shelves lining the walls. The room was always orderly and neat; everything had its place. I would stand next to my mother as she folded with precision and care. She never expected me to help with the folding, never gave me a chore. Later, when I left home, I realized I'd never so much as loaded a washing machine or a dishwasher. My mother had always done everything for me.

As a child, I followed her everywhere. I didn't like to let her out of my sight. Even when she took a bath, I'd stand at her side. I remember the thick, bright red caesarian scar that stood up in a ridge from her pale skin, running from above her belly button all the way down her abdomen. If I asked her about the scar, she'd tell me that it was from my birth and that she was prone to keloid scars—where the scar tissue doesn't fade—and that's why it looked that way.

About once a month, she brushed Clairol's Loving Care hair dye into her glossy black hair, paying special attention to a streak of gray by her part. I would sit next to her in the bathroom as she did this, the ammonia pinching in my throat and nose. She always used Jergens lotion on her hands, which she kept with her powder puff and red and coral lipsticks in golden tubes. At night, I'd watch as she wound her hair into pin curls, fixing each section into a neat loop and securing it with bobby pins.

Even at night, I made sure I wasn't separated from her for long. She'd put me to bed in my own room, but I often woke up at night; I didn't like the dark, and the Dream House made me fearful; I could hear noises outside—the wind, some bird or animal scuffling in the trees—and so I'd get out of my bed and go to her. I remember tiptoeing out of my room in my nightgown, careful not to wake my sisters, whose bedrooms were next to mine. Then I'd walk across to the other side of the house, where my parents slept, pushing gently on the door to their bedroom. My mother and father slept separately, in twin beds with a heavy round marble table between them. The coverlets on their beds were a blue-and-white pattern that was rough and not soft at all.

I was scared of my father; he lost his temper easily, I didn't want to wake him. Often I would curl up in an alcove in their suite, surrounded by books, listening to the sounds of my parents breathing. Sometimes I lay down on the floor next to them. Other times I went to my mother's side and quietly begged her to get up and come with me to my bed. If I accidentally woke my father he'd say angrily, "Oh, Carolyn, tell her to go back to her own room!" But my mother never did tell me. Instead, she'd get up, and together we'd walk hand in hand to my bed. I recall her slow movements and her hushed voice, getting under the warm covers with her. Then she would hold me, we were together, and I would fall right back to sleep. My mother slept with me in my bed most nights until I was ten years old.

Looking back, I wonder if my mother was also awake in the night, and that's why she was always ready to come and sleep in my room with me. Or maybe she needed to get away from my father. Or perhaps she did it for a simpler reason: she wanted someone to hold in the darkness as much as I did.

I KNEW MY MOTHER had been a model when she was younger, but by the time I was born, she had given up her career. It was so hard for me to imagine her life before I came along. She didn't have any old magazines or photos from her time as a model around the house; she explained that she had lost her portfolio on an airplane many years ago. She never told us stories about her career, and although she was always perfectly turned out, her face powered and with a neat coral-colored lip, she rarely got dressed up to go out to parties anymore. In those days, she was simply my mother, moving so dutifully through the tasks of her day—the cooking, the cleaning, the driving, the laundering. My parents didn't have any old friends who came to visit to tell me about how life used to be. Occasionally, my father would tell stories about life during their Manhattan days, the clubs and parties they'd attended, but these usually took the form of jokes, often at my mother's expense.

The only photographs that we had from the past were kept in the cabinet under the dry sink in the den. They were thrown in there randomly, one on top of the other, their edges bent and curling, as if my mother were trying her best to forget about them. I would go there sometimes to look at the black-and-white prints and the faded color ones with the white deckled edges, snapshots of another world. Here were the pictures taken of my mother at Grace's wedding, wearing the wide-brimmed hat and the dress that looked perfectly white in the photographs, but that I knew was actually palest yellow. There was a group shot of Grace with her bridesmaids and flower girls, and one of my mother and Grace sitting at a small table at the wedding reception. Other photographs showed my sister Jill with Grace's daughter, Princess Caroline, both girls dressed up in Sunday best with big bows in their hair. Jill was about ten; Caroline was about four years old. The photos were taken the day my mother drove Jill into the city to meet Grace so they could go together to the ballet.

Then there were my mother's old comp cards, the ones she used to hand out to clients in her modeling days. I loved the comp cards, or "composites," as my mother called them. They listed her height, the size of her waist and bust, her glove size, and her shoe size. And they showed a photo of my mother the model dressed in a fitted suit and a hat, looking up at the windows of Lord & Taylor's department store. In the store window, there was another photo of my mother, this time wearing a wedding dress and smiling. The cards fascinated me.

Even as a child, I was looking for clues, pulling at the threads of the past, trying to picture the person she'd been. I loved spending time looking through the dresser upstairs in my parents' suite filled with all her beautiful things from long ago, her white gloves, the short ones and the long ones for the evenings, her pretty beaded evening bags and her strings of pearls. Then I'd try them on, looking at myself in the mirror, imagining I was a model, too. My mother's closet was still full of all the beautiful gowns she used to wear. I'd run my fingers over the satins, silk, and fur, wondering if she'd ever wear them again. In among the taffeta cocktail dresses and evening coats, I'd seek out the yellow chiffon bridesmaid's dress she'd worn to Princess Grace's wedding in Monaco, the fabric crisp and slightly rough beneath my fingertips.

I knew that Grace had been one of my mother's closest friends when she still lived in Manhattan. But by the time I was born, Grace had moved to Monaco, and although she had come to visit me when I was a baby, she hadn't been back to see us since. Instead, she sent letters and packages for my mother and for my sister Jill, who was her godchild. In one of my earliest memories I'm watching Jill open a birthday gift in a box tied up with long satin ribbons sent by Aunt Grace from the palace in Monaco. I remember my sister searching through layers and layers of tissue paper in the gift box, then pull- ing out two black dresses trimmed with yellow, one tiny and an- other much bigger. My mother explained that Grace had hand-sewn these matching dresses for Jill and her doll to wear. I was so im- pressed, and a little envious of my sister's special gift.

My mother told me that I had a godmother, too. Her name was Sally Richardson, and she was another close friend of Grace's and a bridesmaid along with my mother. After I was born, Sally had given me a special bracelet that was gold with hearts and shooting stars made from diamonds and rubies, which my mother kept in her jew- elry drawer. I could remember meeting Sally once, going to her apartment in Manhattan. While we were there, my mother was tense, distracted. Later, she told me that she thought Sally was up- set because we didn't send a thank-you note for the gift of the brace- let. The story always made me feel ashamed.

I wondered if Grace felt the same way about the gifts for Jill. Maybe that was why the princess hadn't been to visit us.

CHAPTER 3

Carolyn

In order to picture Grace as my mother first saw her in November 1947, you have to put aside the images of the blond movie star or the perfect princess on her Monaco wedding day. Instead, you have to see her as a round-faced teenage girl with light brown wavy hair. She's stepping out of the Barbizon's revolving doors on Sixty-third Street in New York City, wearing a little black coat with a matching hat decorated with a sprig of blue flowers.

Carolyn watched as the girl sent the hotel's revolving doors spinning behind her, her black high heels clicking as she went.

How pretty she is, Carolyn thought, *and how well dressed.*

The next time Carolyn saw the girl, she was leaving her room on the ninth floor, right next door to Carolyn's. It turned out they were neighbors.

The girl introduced herself. She was Grace, from Philadelphia, and she was studying acting at the nearby American Academy of Dramatic Arts.

Now that introductions had been made, Carolyn and Grace kept running into each other, in the hotel hallways, in the elevators, while waiting for the shared bathrooms, at the diner in the lobby downstairs.

Carolyn learned that although Grace was almost a year younger, at eighteen, when it came to New York, she was an old hand. She had started her first semester at the Academy in September, so had been living at the Barbizon two months by the time Carolyn arrived. She had an uncle who lived in Manhattan, who was a playwright, who also directed plays, and even when Grace was still in Philadelphia, she often came to visit him to go to the latest shows. Grace was in love with Broadway and the theater. She knew the names of every show currently playing in New York and every actor appearing in them. She collected playbills, pasting her treasured torn ticket stubs in a scrapbook she'd kept since high school, the dates and play names noted in the margins.

Meanwhile, Carolyn followed fashion as closely as Grace followed the theater, making all her own clothes, scrutinizing *Vogue* patterns, adapting them to her own designs. Before coming to New York, she had made herself a black pencil skirt and a black-and-white gingham blouse, with a black patent leather belt and matching gingham gloves complete with a cuff. The gloves were hard to execute, and she could barely wiggle her fingers when she wore them, but the skirt and blouse fit beautifully.

Unlike Carolyn, Grace saw clothes as a means to an end, preferring sensible shoes, which she wore with tweed suits, skirts, and cardigans. Often she tied back her hair with a scarf—it was so fine and would never stay put. She was nearsighted and wore horn-rimmed glasses. At home in Philadelphia, Grace's mother despaired at her daughter's lack of interest in fashion or feminine activities such as sewing or knitting. Whenever Grace started making a dress or a scarf, she would become bored and put it in a drawer before it was finished.

Carolyn was soft-spoken, bordering on shy. Grace was more confident and outgoing, with a talent for impersonations that made her new friend laugh. Yet despite their differences, Grace and Carolyn were drawn together by a shared sense of purpose. They were both in New York to pursue careers and to escape the narrow expectations of their families.

Grace had wanted to be an actress since childhood, but her father, Jack Kelly, disapproved of the theater. Before Grace finished high school earlier in the year, her parents had insisted she apply for college, but she had failed to get a place. There were so many young men coming back from the war, and they were being given priority. After she was turned down by Bennington College, Grace saw her chance. She auditioned for the American Academy of Dramatic Arts and got in. Jack Kelly was not impressed. At college, his daughter might meet a suitable husband, but at a drama school, there was no telling whom she might run into. Initially he refused to give his permission, but eventually Grace wore him down. Jack agreed to let his daughter go to New York on one condition: that she stay at the Barbizon, where she would be safe. Grace's mother, Margaret, reassured Jack that since Grace never stuck at anything, she'd be home in three weeks.

Grace, who had been at the hotel since September by now, had happily already proved her mother's prediction wrong.

Before long, Carolyn and Grace were knocking on each other's doors, sitting on each other's beds, sharing the day. Outside it was one of the coldest New York winters on record, but in their rooms, it was cozy. With Grace's help, Carolyn began learning the city, venturing out in temperatures so sharp they made your temples ache. There was Central Park, the hotel's unofficial backyard, which you reached by walking west, entering through the gates nearest to the children's zoo. Along Fifth Avenue, the city's wealthiest residents stepped in and out of gleaming storefronts. If you kept walking east, beyond Lexington to Third Avenue, you entered another universe filled with antiques shops and old-world restaurants opened by refugees from the war.

Carolyn loved the way that when you returned to the hotel Oscar, the smiling doorman, would always be waiting in his smart blue uniform and cap to welcome you home. He was bald and jowly under the hat that he tipped to each one of the guests as they passed. Legend had it that he had arrived at the Barbizon the year after it opened in 1927 and had been standing under the awning at Sixty-third Street ever since. Nothing seemed to make Oscar happier than saluting the hotel's residents as they left the building, handing them into taxicabs as if they were princesses or movie stars, waving them on their way, then welcoming them back as if he hadn't seen them in years. For Carolyn, Oscar was the opposite of her stepfather, welcoming her home with bolts across the door.

IN THE COMING WEEKS, Carolyn left the Barbizon in the mornings with new conviction. She had taken the young photographer's advice and had signed with the Harry Conover agency on Vanderbilt Avenue, twenty blocks from the hotel. Conover was a former male model, with slicked-back jet-black hair and a salesman's smile, whose agency supplied girls to photographers, advertising agencies, department stores, fashion shows, movie scouts, and publicity agents.

Carolyn was petite at five feet four, not tall enough for high fashion, but Conover could see her potential as a junior model. "Junior" clothing lines aimed specifically at teenagers were a relatively new phenomenon. Before the war, young women had worn the same clothing and read the same magazines as their mothers. But now that clothing rationing was finally over, manufacturers had discovered a new and lucrative youth market. Magazines like *Seventeen*, *Charm*, and *Junior Bazaar* showed their teenage readers a world of sweaters and skirts, bobby socks and loafers, boyfriends, slumber parties, and the hit parade. Carolyn's prettiness, so effortless, relatable, and girl-next-door, fit with this vision.

Conover was going to show Carolyn's photographs to interested clients, and in return, he'd keep 10 percent of her fee when she booked a job. Starting out, her hourly rate would be five dollars; the rest was up to her. If she was serious about becoming a successful model, she was going to have to work for it. There were plenty of beautiful young girls in New York, Conover warned. What separated you from the pack was determination. You had to go door to door and office to office, receptionist to receptionist, introducing yourself to photographers and advertising clients, campaigning as you went.

Each day, Conover would send Carolyn a new list of appointments, with the addresses of photographers and agencies looking for junior girls. Then Carolyn took out her map of New York and started walking. She entered unfamiliar lobbies, ascended into darkened stairwells, or took elevators into unknown buildings, never knowing exactly where she was going and what would be waiting for her there. It took a lot of pluck to keep walking into those lobbies and stairwells and elevators, but Carolyn knew she either succeeded as a model or she went back to Steubenville.

More often than not, there would be a gaggle of pretty girls waiting in the reception area by the time she arrived. Soon enough, small groups of girls were called into a room where the clients were waiting. The clients were almost always men, sometimes as many as four of them sitting wordlessly at a desk. After the girls handed over their test shots, they stood in a line in the middle of the room, positioning themselves at different angles, while the men behind the desk looked them up and down.

Then the critique would begin, with the clients discussing each girl's merits and flaws among themselves. Carolyn got to know her body and its shortcomings very quickly—and all the other girls' imperfections, too. One model, Eleanor, had ears that stuck out, and she had them pinned back. Another had freckles and had to have an abrasive treatment to remove them. Carolyn had circles under her eyes, which she soon learned to cover with makeup.

After the assessment was over, either Carolyn would get booked for the job or she wouldn't, and there was no way of knowing why she had or hadn't been chosen. Much of it seemed to depend on the mood of the clients—whether one of them had had an

argument with his wife or girlfriend and somehow you reminded him of her.

At the end of the day, Carolyn went back to the hotel and waited for the phone by her bed to ring.

And it did. Her first modeling job was a two-page spread, for *Junior Bazaar*, a magazine aimed at the twelve-to-twenty-year-old set.

The theme of the shoot was "youthful fashion at an affordable price," and it featured Carolyn and two other models standing against a giant white backdrop with an ironing board, an iron, a laundry basket, and a hamper filled with clothes. For the next few hours, the models posed as laundresses, carrying, folding, and pressing laundry. Carolyn had two looks in the final spread. One was a gray cotton lawn dress "with baby sleeves, tied into little puffs and a very deep ruffle around the hemline." The other was "sand-colored pillow ticking, striped in thin lines of white, with a trim Eton jacket and a cummerbund skirt pinch-pleated all the way around." In one of her photographs, Carolyn looks down, examining her iron pensively, assessing it for the correct heat. In another, she's playfully hitched her dress over the ironing board while wearing it, so that another model can press her skirt, as if such duties were in fact every young girl's dream.

Before long, she was modeling in advertisements for junior fashion lines, wearing sundresses, playsuits, and nightgowns.

On one of her shoots, Carolyn ran into the young photographer who'd introduced her to Conover. She told him that thanks to him, her career had officially begun. The photographer smiled and asked her if she'd like to go away with him for the weekend, as if she owed him something for his help. Carolyn was horrified. She told him no, that she wasn't that kind of girl, that they hadn't even been on a date together! Then she quickly made her excuses and fled back to Sixty-third Street, where Oscar the doorman waited, hat tipping as she flew through the revolving doors, into the lobby, across to the elevator, and up to her room, where no man could follow.

IT WAS CAROLYN's first Christmas in New York. Grace went home to Philadelphia, to be with her family, but Carolyn had worked so hard to get to Manhattan that she couldn't afford to leave just yet. On Christmas Day, a blizzard began to swirl outside her hotel window, and when she woke up the following morning, New York was covered in white. Cars and buses were stalled in the streets, and the subways were halted. The city was silent; the only occasional sound was the scraping of a superintendent's shovel making a path along the sidewalk. Dark gray clouds blotted the sun. In the space of less than twenty-four hours, the snowfall had reached almost twenty-six inches.

In the afternoons, she joined the other hotel-bound residents on the mezzanine for company and the complimentary afternoon tea. She wasn't the only one who stayed on at the hotel over the holidays. There were girls from Michigan and Texas, Illinois and Arizona—so many others who had come too far to go home, girls who were here in New York to pursue all kinds of careers, as nurse's aides, dental assistants, bookkeepers, receptionists, and hat-check girls. There was even one young woman who had qualified as a carpenter, obtaining her union card.

Thanks to Mrs. Sibley's efficient vetting process at the front desk, most of the Barbizon girls were still in their teens and early twenties, but there was a small group of older residents who always came out of their rooms around teatime, lured by the complimentary cookies. These were the Barbizon ladies, some of them in their forties and even fifties. They were women who had arrived in the city during their younger years but who had never married and so had never left; some of them had been at the hotel since it opened in 1927, twenty years ago. The younger girls shuddered to think of it. Imagine never leaving this place! The Barbizon was fine for a bit of an adventure, just as long as you didn't have to stay forever. You wanted the hotel's revolving doors to spin you out *into* the city, not back into the lobby again.

CHAPTER 4

Nina

When I was a child, my mother often took me into Manhattan. She didn't trust the doctors on Long Island, so we would always drive into New York for my appointments. In photographs from that time I'm a thin and pale-faced child with dark circles under my eyes; I never seemed to have rosy cheeks. I was prone to stomachaches, fatigue, sore throats, strep infections, all kinds of ailments and illnesses. From a young age, I knew the city was the place you went to be rescued, to be made better again.

At the wheel, my mother smoked with the window cracked, tapping her cigarette into the pull-out ashtray. I sat quietly at her side, looking out, wondering what the doctors would say this time. I was accustomed to the examining rooms, with their bright lighting and silvery equipment. I knew all about wearing the little cotton gown, sitting on a tall chair with my legs swinging while the nurse took my blood pressure and the doctor pressed a cold hard stethoscope to my back. I was very good at sitting still and sticking out my tongue; I'd had a lot of practice. My father once told me my mother had taken me to as many as fifty doctors in a single year.

The problem was that each doctor we visited usually sent us home with a pat on the shoulder and the reassurance that everything would be just fine, that I would get better soon. My mother wasn't so easily convinced. We would have to see the next doctor and then another. We were always looking for the right test, the right medicine; the miracle cure.

After each appointment was over, if I was lucky, my mother would take me to the doll hospital on Lexington Avenue as a reward for being a good girl. I had one particular Tabitha doll that I loved. The doll was modeled on Elizabeth Montgomery's daughter from the TV show *Bewitched*. Like me, my Tabitha was often sick; I knew I needed to take good care of her. The doll hospital was upstairs on the second floor, a brightly lit workshop where doll doctors operated on dolls from little wooden workbenches. On the shelves were hundreds of dolls that had been brought to be mended, some new, some old, some small, some nearly as big as me. Then there were stacks of boxes for doll parts neatly labeled "hands," "fingers," "wrists," "wigs," and "German eyes," "French eyes," and "American eyes." I'd carefully give my Tabitha doll to the chief surgeon, and after a little while, Tabitha would be given back to me, good as new.

As a child, I knew I wasn't so easily fixed.

My mother had told me that I had internal bleeding. It was a concept that terrified me; I imagined the blood escaping my veins and seeping throughout my entire body. Once I had blood in my stool, and this was enough to convince her that something was seriously wrong with me. She also explained to me I was anemic. It was true that I was pale and easily became out of breath.

MY FATHER HAD another daughter, Patricia, from his first marriage. Patricia was my blond, glamorous, and grown-up half sister, twenty years older than I. She worked for my father's friend Sherman as his executive secretary, and she lived in an apartment in Manhattan. Patricia would come to visit us on the weekends or holidays, bringing her city friends with her. Once she brought along Dori, who had been her roommate for a while. Dori was a model, and this got my attention because I knew my mother had been a model before I was born. Dori wore a pink scarf in her soft dark brown hair that fell in strands around her face like a halo; I thought she was so beautiful. I wanted to spend time with her. She and I sat together in the mustard-colored wide-wale corduroy chair in our den and had our picture taken. I had recently gotten a short pixie haircut, and I wore a pale-pink-and-navy-striped short-sleeved turtleneck and navy pants. Dori said that our outfits matched.

I learned that Dori was married and her husband was a very successful ear, nose, and throat doctor practicing in New York City. My mother seized on the opportunity to tell Dori all about my sore throats. Dori agreed to help us. Soon after, my mother took me into the city to see Dori's husband, Dr. Schneider, at his offices. He told us I had two areas of staph infection on my adenoids left over from when I had my tonsils removed. I was going to have to have surgery. We began planning for the hospital stay immediately. The surgery was scheduled at Lenox Hill Hospital on the Upper East Side of Manhattan. My mother seemed relieved. Finally, we had a diagnosis and something to do.

After I came home from the surgery, my sore throats got better, but other problems replaced them.

MY SCHOOL RECORDS tell the story of my mother's ongoing concern for my health. The first one I have is from kindergarten, November 1964, when I was about to turn five.

"Mrs. Reybold quite concerned with child's progress in school," my teacher wrote. "Nina had to have a hernia operation early in the year. Nina is a lovely, sensitive little girl. Enjoys playing with dolls from home a great deal. Tires easily and often cannot complete a project. Tends to play alone or perhaps with one other child. Nina has missed quite a bit of school due to numerous strep infections. Her attendance is not consistent, making it difficult especially in the readiness program. She seems to be a capable little girl if she had the proper background in the readiness program."

By April of the following year, my report states that my teachers were considering holding me back, as my lack of attendance meant I was struggling to keep up.

Halfway through first grade, the school reports make clear that my progress was being severely limited by my prolonged absences. By February of 1966, I had been absent for about half the school days in the report period. The school requested that my primary physician fill out a physical examination form confirming my ongoing health problems. Then, in June of 1966, my mother failed to appear at my parent-teacher conference. "There have been numerous attempts made to have a conference with Mrs. Reybold," my teacher wrote, "and all attempts have failed. Nina's attendance has been very poor. As a result, she has learned very little this year. Better luck next year!"

According to the school reports, I'd had a tonsillectomy and adenoidectomy in first grade, which would have explained why I needed to take at least a few days away from my classes. But why so many other days missed?

The following year, the reports show that I had a "gastrointestinal series," and this I remember well. It led to yet another test: this time a barium enema, so the doctors would be able to take an X-ray and see if there was anything wrong with my colon. The pain of the barium injection in my rectum was so excruciating I was given codeine after the procedure, which only made me throw up. Afterward, the X-ray showed no abnormalities.

My mother told the school I needed further tests and X-rays and that a note would be forthcoming from our doctor advising the school of my condition.

When I was almost seven, a doctor from Suffolk County School District No. 2 examined me.

"Nina Reybold was examined on 10.10.66," the doctor wrote. "She was found in good general health and able to participate in all athletic programs, required and intra-mural curricular. No recommendations or exceptions."

At this point, my mother must have felt encouraged to send me back to school, because at my parent-teacher conference in November, my teacher reported that "Mrs. Reybold is very pleased with Nina's progress this year. She says Nina is very interested in books at home—often reading. I am very pleased with Nina's progress in all areas. She has come out of her shell and is interested in everything we do at school. She is a conscientious worker and this is proving to make her very successful. I am very pleased with her attitudes, and find her an asset to the class."

But by June of second grade I had been absent so much that my teachers couldn't comment on my reading record.

So many days I stayed home from school, resting in my bedroom. Mine was the smallest of the three bedrooms in the wing I shared with my sisters. It had slanted high ceilings and a large picture window that faced the garage. The furniture was white, with a canopy four-poster bed and a white bedspread with red eyelet trim. Here I played with my dolls and read my books.

My sister Jill was the one who got me interested in reading, giving me my first Nancy Drew, *The Secret of the Old Clock*. After that, I begged my mother to buy me each additional book in the series so that I could read them all. I loved the Nancy books with their familiar black-and-yellow spines and the brave girl detective whose life was so boldly different from mine. I'd been in school just enough to get the hang of reading, but after Jill gave me the confidence to read on my own, I started going to the library and coming home with stacks of books. I fell in love with reading, filling the long hours of my days with the stories I found in the pages.

I also watched a lot of TV. In my room, I had a small black-and-white television with a rabbit-ear antenna on the top, or I would go downstairs and watch TV in the den. I was addicted to soap operas. My favorites were *Dark Shadows* and *General Hospital*. I became attached to the characters and to their dramas. In the soap operas, children found out that their parents weren't their parents. Husbands who seemed trustworthy turned out to be cheating on their wives. Siblings stopped talking to one another and stabbed each other in the back. In my own family, tensions simmered below the surface, exploding into arguments in ways I couldn't understand. In the world of soap operas, the drama was constant and easy to predict. Drinks were thrown in faces, doors were slammed, cars sped away into the night, and everyone said exactly what they thought. You could depend on the characters to be as hurt, angry, and vocal as yesterday, and always at the regularly scheduled time.

News broadcasts also helped to break up the day. I watched the news on ABC religiously at 7:00 A.M., 5:00 P.M., and 11:00 P.M. I loved the handsome newscasters for their firmness, their solemn voices, and their confidence. Bill Beutel and Roger Grimsby were my heroes; no matter what happened, they took the world as they found it and explained it in terms even a child could understand. Back then every night on the news, they would read the body count from the war in Vietnam. Across the country, people were marching and protesting, against the war, for civil rights. I remember when Martin Luther King was shot in Memphis, watching the news, seeing Robert Kennedy standing up on the back of a flatbed truck, urging for calm and unity in King's memory. When two months later Kennedy was also shot and killed, it seemed as if the violence would never end. At home in my room, in my bed, via the little box of my television, I had a window on the strangeness of the world.

If my mother allowed it—if I was well enough and the weather was warm—I was allowed to wander through the woods at the back of our house through the tangled honeysuckle and raspberry bushes that grew on the property. On weekends I might go to play with Fay, the daughter of Sherman's groundskeeper, who lived next door to the castle and who was two years older than I. But during the weekdays I was mostly alone or with my cat, Little. Little was a gray cat with white mitten paws, and everywhere I went, she would follow me. We'd play hide-and-go-seek in the cattails on our beach. I talked to Little; she was my friend; sometimes I thought she knew what I was thinking. Then we'd wander out onto our beach at the back of our house with its mottled sand, pitted with grasses and a small inlet, looking out across the gray waters of the Sound. There I'd sit on a rock and pretend I was someone else: a princess waiting to be rescued by a prince, or a famous model like my mother. Then, when the light started to ebb out of the sky, I'd go back to the house to see what the evening would bring.

Years later, I reconnected with the daughter of one of our neighbors on Long Island. She told me that she would often ride her bike by our house, to see if she could catch a glimpse of me at the window. "We knew there was a strange girl who lived there but she mostly stayed in her room because she was sickly," our neighbor told me. "It was like a mystery—what was going on in there?"

CHAPTER 5

Carolyn

My mother in her Barbizon days is a person I barely recognize: so excited, happy, and hopeful, standing at the window of her hotel room looking out over a city that she felt was hers for the taking. She was so completely alone in New York, without any family support or a built-in safety net, yet determined not only to survive but to succeed.

In the evenings, both Carolyn and Grace did their homework. Carolyn wrote the next day's modeling appointments in her notebook, scrutinizing her map of Manhattan, so she would know exactly where to go and what time to leave to get there. Then she practiced smoothing her hair and applying her makeup with care. Her looks were her currency: her even features, the satin of her hair, the slender figure and tiny waist—these had been her ticket out of Steubenville, and now they were going to be her means of staying in New York. Her appearance might have been her birthright, but Carolyn knew it was up to her to convert it into a career.

Grace was also fighting for a self-made place in the world. Unlike Carolyn, Grace came from money—her father was a millionaire—but that wouldn't help her if she failed in New York; she'd still have no place to go but back home. Each night, after her classes at the Academy were over, Grace practiced her vocal exercises standing in front of a mirror in her room, a clothespin on her nose. Her instructors at the Academy had told her that her voice was too high and nasal and "improperly placed." She kept a wire recorder in her room and listened to herself so that she might improve her diction, working to perfect a tone that was lower, with an accent that fell somewhere mid-Atlantic. They were such hard workers, the two of them, building their lives up from scratch in those next-door rooms on the ninth floor.

THE NEXT TIME Carolyn appeared in a magazine, it was in an advertisement for silverware. This time, she wore a canary-yellow dress, with puffed sleeves and a black ribbon at her waist.

Carolyn learned to model on the job, listening to the photographer's direction and observing the other, more experienced girls. For some shoots, clothing was provided, but for others you had to bring your own outfits; you were told in advance whether to come dressed for the street or in afternoon dresses or evening gowns. The other models carried around black bandboxes with a leather strap attached where you could store an extra change of clothes and accessories, so Carolyn started carrying a bandbox, too. Instinctively, she understood how to dress a look up or down, adding a jacket, a hat, or an apron, or changing shoes. The photographers appreciated her ability to style herself, delivering exactly whatever the job required.

Carolyn kept booking jobs, and the more jobs she booked, the

more photographs she had to circulate to prospective clients, which meant more assignments. Each new appointment was scrawled on the callboard marked CAROLYN SCHAFFNER in the Conover offices. After only three months in New York, Carolyn had appeared in *Glamour, Junior Bazaar, Seventeen, Mademoiselle,* and *Charm*. By now, she was making more than enough money to cover her expenses, but even so, she worried about paying her weekly bill at the Barbizon. The reality was that Conover was slow to pay. He had hundreds of models on his books and seemed to barely know their names, let alone how much he owed them. Two months after Carolyn started work for him, she was still waiting for Conover to cut her a check.

Carolyn wasn't the only model unhappy with Conover's failure to pay. Many of the girls were talking about a new agency started the year before by the model Natálie Nickerson and her friend Eileen Ford. Natálie was one of the most successful and highly paid models in New York. Blond and towering at five feet ten, she'd initially been with John Robert Powers—another well-established New York modeling agency—but had left in protest after Powers repeatedly failed to pay her on time. Natálie had heard about models in California who were taking matters into their own hands, asking clients to pay them directly. So she set up her own shop with Eileen, a former model booker. Together, the two women had instituted a new payment method. At the end of each job, the model gave an invoice to the photographer, and then the photographer paid the girl directly. After that, the model paid the agency its 10 percent fee. Instead of waiting months to be paid, the model got her money right away.

Natálie had heard about Carolyn's success as a junior model and suggested to Eileen that they approach her about joining their fledgling agency. And so, one morning in the new year, Carolyn found herself walking across to Eileen's offices on Second Avenue in the Fifties. Arriving at the dilapidated old brownstone sandwiched between a funeral parlor and a cigar store, Carolyn had to check to make sure she had the correct address. After she confirmed she was in the right place, she rang the bell and went inside, climbing the darkened stairs, then knocking on a red-painted door on the third floor. A voice called out to her to come in, and Carolyn peered around the door, looking for a receptionist's desk or banks of secretaries. Instead, a tiny woman with a shock of curly brown hair sat in a small room at a folding card table, in front of six black telephones, one of the receivers tucked under her chin.

This was Eileen.

Carolyn sat on the office's old red sofa while Eileen explained, rapid-fire, how the agency worked. While Natálie was the "face" of the agency, bringing new girls into the fold, Eileen handled the business side, fielding the phone calls, negotiating with the clients, and taking the photographers to task when they failed to pay or made unwanted approaches to her girls. Like Natálie, Eileen was in her early twenties, not much older than many of the young women she represented. She understood the models on her books, knew what they needed from her. At most agencies, models were responsible for every aspect of the job—all the footwork, selling yourself, figuring out where you had to be and when, bringing the right clothing and makeup to the shoot. There was no training, no instruction, and very little support. The girls worked hard for the agency, but the agency gave very little in return. Natálie and Eileen felt that these male agents had gotten things upside down: the agent should work for the model, not the other way around. Eileen saw her role as overseeing every aspect of a model's career, from how a girl styled her hair to how she moved in front of the camera to the rates she could command.

Eileen understood the junior market well. She had helped style the cover for the very first issue of *Seventeen* in 1944. After that, she went to work as a model booker for Bill Becker's photographic studio, the biggest commercial photography studio in the United States. Next she'd worked for the Arnold Constable department store, hiring models for their advertisements and catalogs, negotiating fiercely with the major agencies like Conover and Powers. She knew the business from every angle.

She was also protective.

"No girl on my books will ever be allowed to model lingerie, or appear in cheesecake or bathtub shots," Eileen declared.

Carolyn felt sure that with Eileen, she would be in excellent hands. Eileen was aware that the teenage market was growing and that she needed more junior models on the books. Carolyn was fresh-faced and petite and had the exact attributes that Eileen was looking for in any girl: wide eyes that photographed well in any kind of light; a straight nose, narrow at the bridge; a physique that was naturally slender; a small waist. Before Eileen would book Carolyn for a job, however, they needed to make one tweak. The problem was her last name. Schaffner was "too ethnic," too Steubenville, Eileen explained. Carolyn needed something more sophisticated. "Scott" was perfect—short and to the point. And so Carolyn Schaffner became Carolyn Scott.

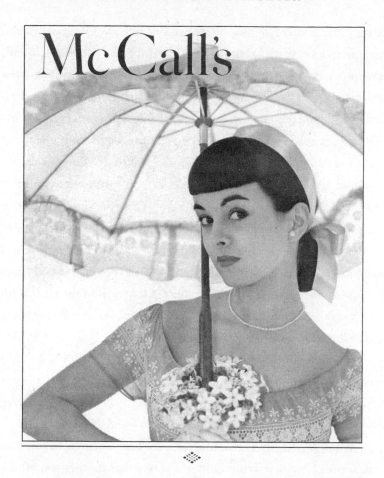

One of the first jobs Eileen secured for Carolyn Scott was a cover shoot for *McCall's*, a glossy monthly women's magazine with a readership of nearly 4 million. The photographer was Richard Avedon, a young New Yorker with dark thick-rimmed glasses, whom Eileen referred to fondly as "Dickie." Dickie was twenty-five at the time, and an up-and-comer. The previous year, he'd photographed Natálie Nickerson for his first *Harper's Bazaar* cover. Since then, he had gained a reputation around the agency for treating the models better than any other photographer in town. While most of the photographers treated the girls like cattle, to be prodded around, Avedon made the girls feel appreciated. He played music during the shoots, letting the models pick out albums from his collection; he ordered the girls their favorite food to eat. He saw models as his collaborators as much as his subjects, and they loved him for it.

In the cover photograph Avedon took for *McCall's,* Carolyn's outfit and pose are demure, but the look in her eyes is more complex— provocative and questioning. Avedon saw in Carolyn something that no one had noticed before in the girl from Steubenville: her intelligence.

With Eileen's representation, Carolyn began securing more and more jobs, her fees went up, and she was finally getting paid on time. She had done it. She had secured a place for herself in the city. With the money from her modeling jobs, she knew she could stay on at the Barbizon for the indefinite future.

There was so little she missed about Steubenville, but that didn't mean she didn't often think of her mother, Dorothy, still at home in the clapboard house on Pennsylvania Avenue. Dorothy's days were filled with the labors of taking care of a husband and two children, now without her older daughter to help her. Carolyn decided to take some of her newfound money and send her mother something to help make her life just a little easier. Back home, Dorothy still cooled the milk and butter with an ice block in the larder—and the milk often soured and went to waste. So Carolyn arranged for the latest model of refrigerator to be sent home to Ohio.

As THE WEEKS went on, Grace started to see something in Carolyn's growing financial independence that she coveted. Yes, Grace was fortunate to have a father who paid her way and took care of all her needs, sending checks to the Barbizon and the American Academy of Dramatic Arts to cover her room and tuition each month. But there was a downside to Grace's family support. Jack Kelly was determined to control and dominate his daughter's every decision. It was Jack who had insisted that Grace stay at the Barbizon; Jack who had pointed out that she never succeeded at anything and would likely return home again after three weeks in New York. Jack was paying her way, but this meant that he maintained the power, and this put Grace's ambitions at risk. She knew that if for any reason her father decided to withdraw funding for her studies, she'd be forced to return to Philadelphia. Meanwhile, Carolyn paid her own way and answered to no one.

It was Carolyn who suggested Grace try modeling. She had seen Grace at the hotel, coming back from the shared bathrooms along the hallway, her face wiped clean each evening. She saw the perfect symmetry of her features, the beauty behind the glasses and the headscarves that Grace wore during the day to her classes at the Academy. She felt Grace had potential as a model, so she sent her to see Eileen. Like Carolyn before her, Grace climbed the two flights of stairs to Eileen's offices and sat on the red sofa, waiting to be appraised. But Eileen wasn't impressed. Eileen felt Grace wasn't slender enough, was too commercial for her stable. "Too much meat on the bones," Eileen later explained. In years to come, Eileen would admit that saying no to the young Grace Kelly was the biggest mistake of her career.

Fortunately, Grace had other connections. Her mother had once modeled for the John Robert Powers Agency, and after being turned down by Eileen, Grace went directly to Powers, who took her on right away. Her first modeling job was a television commercial for

Bridgeport Brass pesticide, requiring her to run around the room spraying at imaginary insects. More jobs quickly followed.

WITH THEIR HARD-EARNED money in their pockets, the girls could afford to have interests. Thanks to her affiliation with the Academy, Grace was able to purchase inexpensive tickets to the shows on Broadway, so they could go to plays and musicals whenever they liked. They started buying tickets for the ballet, too. It was 1948, and the New York City Ballet was in its first season at City Center, only a few blocks from the hotel. They went there whenever they could, falling in love with George Balanchine's beautiful, long-legged dancers—Maria Tallchief, Marie-Jeanne, Tanaquil Le Clercq. When they left the theater after nightfall, walking out onto Fifty-fifth Street, they were still under the spell of the costumes and movements, the actual world seeming unreal compared to the visions they'd just left behind them.

If they wanted to extend the fantasy, Carolyn and Grace would walk over to the Russian Tea Room on Fifty-seventh Street, with its mural of the ballerinas of the Ballet Russe in *Les Sylphides* and *Swan Lake* on every side. At the neighboring tables, they could hear the chatter of Russian émigrés, exiled by revolution and war. And if they stayed late enough after one of the performances, they might glimpse Mr. Balanchine himself, walking in through the glass doors of the restaurant with a ballerina on either arm, at which point the entire room would erupt in applause.

For two girls in love with the ballet, New York in 1948 was a wonderful place. The Ballet Russe de Monte Carlo was still based in Manhattan, as it had been since the war. The Ballet Theatre was at Rockefeller Center. The film *The Red Shoes* had just opened its run at the Bijou Theatre on Forty-fifth Street. Grace and Carolyn went as soon as they could, their eyes swimming with the new Technicolor, with its vivid greens, reds, and blues. Growing up in Steubenville, Carolyn had always wanted to take dance classes, but her stepfather wouldn't allow it. He put his foot down, said they didn't have the money to waste. Now that she was in New York, Carolyn had her own money and could spend it as she wished. She signed up for

classes in the Balanchine method at a nearby dance school and started going to weekly classes. She loved her lessons, the teacher's insistence on precision and control. She learned that a simple stretch of the foot and leg—a *tendu*—wasn't just an isolated movement; it was part of an artistic journey that expressed something about how you *felt*. You practiced the same stretch over and over, pointing your toe directly ahead of you, then to the side and behind, dozens of times, until the movements became second nature.

In classes, Carolyn moved well; she had a natural grace. She thought about dancing professionally, but her teachers warned her it was already too late. She had just turned twenty, and most dancers of a similar age had been training for a decade or more. So Carolyn took what she had learned and applied it to her work as a model. By November of 1948, when she was photographed by Francesco Scavullo for a six-page feature in *Seventeen* wearing a party dress of velvet and rayon taffeta, her tiny waist nipped by a bow, she stands with a dancer's carriage, her leg positioned elegantly behind her in a perfect *tendu*.

CHAPTER 6

Nina

Whereas my mother was always there with me when I was growing up, like the waters of the Sound with its thin strip of beach, my father was like the weather: he came and went, and you never knew how it would be tomorrow.

Like so many other fathers of his generation, he was almost completely uninvolved in anything to do with his children. I don't remember him ever going to a parent-teacher conference, or helping me with my schoolwork, or even commenting on the fact that I was so often at home sick in bed. During the week, he stayed in the city, and on the weekends, when he came home, he spent most of his time next door with his friend Sherman. He was much older than my mother, entering his fifties when I was born. It was as if he inhabited another world, one filled with his own interests, work, and social activities; a world that had nothing to do with my mother's chores, with children, or with the slow ticking clock of our days.

It's hard for me to remember any more than a handful of instances when my father paid me any real attention during my childhood. I usually kept quiet, didn't make a fuss like my sisters, and as a result, I rarely caught his interest. Occasionally, he would allow me to come and sit with him in the den to watch TV. Here he had a special storage unit for his beloved RCA television set, including a wooden tray that slid out that he had designed himself. I would sit on the dark blue corduroy-covered sofa, and he would sit opposite, sunk deep into his comfortable black chair, in front of his fully stocked bar and his library wall with his books, watching the flickering color TV.

On the walls of the den, my father hung his collection of paintings and reproductions from his family archives. He was originally from Georgia, and despite spending most of his adult life in the North, he maintained his accent and his pride in his southern heritage. (According to my father, our Georgian ancestors were responsible for bringing peaches to the United States.) I remember a print of *George Washington Crossing the Delaware* that hung in a thick gilt frame above the couch. Then there was the black-and-white photo of a steamboat, the *Major Philip Reybold,* built by one of my father's ancestors in the 1850s. The story went that one stormy night the steamboat was out on the Delaware River when it was struck by a tornado and the ship's silver bell was lost. According to local legend, whenever severe weather threatened the waters of the Delaware, you could hear the *Reybold* bell ringing out from the depths of the river.

Only once do I remember my father asking me to join him in any other activity at the house besides watching TV. I was in the kitchen with my mother, and I could hear him calling for me. It was early summer, and he wanted me to come outside to help him plant some marigolds. My father loved to garden, and he did all of the landscaping around the house himself. He built a grape arbor trellis that led all the way along a brick path from the kitchen to the garage; there were beds of green pachysandra all along the front of the house and to either side; in summer, I remember rhododendron bushes and white petunias with red snapdragons, and pink petunias outside the kitchen. I was so honored that he would trust me with the task of planting the marigolds that I got up from the table go to him, but my mother stood in my way. I wasn't well enough, she explained. I needed to stay inside. The marigold beds were on the opposite side of the house, too far away from the kitchen windows she could look out of to check on me. After a while, my father stopped calling for me. He never asked me to join him in the garden again.

Even when the five of us were home together, we kept to ourselves: my father in his den or in the garden; my mother and me in the laundry room or the kitchen; my sisters in their rooms. The only time I remember going someplace as a family was to the Fireman's Fair in nearby Southdown. I must have been about six years old. The fair was in the parking lot of the firehouse. There were fire trucks on display, a big Ferris wheel, and carnival games for the children. To my delight, my father came with me to play one of the games. I had to throw balls and knock down three clown faces, and, with my father's help, I won. My prize was either a doll or toy cap guns. I chose the cap guns; they were white and silver and came with a belt and holsters. I knew my father had always wanted a son—my baby blanket that I kept for years was blue with a white ribbon trim because my mother had been so convinced she was going to have a boy. I knew I had been a disappointment to him, so I thought perhaps playing with boy toys would help keep his attention just a little bit longer. I was right. My father got a big kick out of my choice. He loved that I chose the guns.

BEFORE I WAS BORN, my father had been a successful advertising executive on Madison Avenue; when I was still a baby, he had worked in publishing for McGraw-Hill. But by the time my memories of him begin, he had left his corporate job to work for himself as an inventor and entrepreneur. His company, the Sight Radio Corporation, had its offices on Park Avenue. My father's big idea was to use the new technology of the "flap display"—the kind you saw in train stations with the numbers and letters on metal flaps that flipped to reveal your platform and departure time—to keep airport travelers up-to-date with the latest news. "Sight Radios" were large freestanding boxes designed to sit in airport lounges with displays that flipped to show the latest weather alerts, sports updates, and news headlines.

In all his ventures, my father was encouraged by the example of his friend and our neighbor Sherman Fairchild. In those days, Sherman was one of the most successful inventors and investors in America. His Fairchild Camera and Instrument Corporation had developed the first aerial camera, the first home movie camera with sound, the first synchronized camera shutter and flash. He had been on the cover of *Time* magazine. Sherman had made millions of dollars from his patents, and he was constantly coming up with new ideas. One day, he was trying to light a cigarette outside, and the match blew out; he set about designing a new and improved match with a slot below the head for air currents to pass through so the flame would stay lit in the breeze.

Throughout my childhood, there was always the expectation that at any moment, my father might achieve a level of success similar to Sherman's and our circumstances might change. He designed drinking glasses with portraits of tennis champions on them. He made a square game table with an inset board that could be turned over to reveal a backgammon board. He pioneered a belt made from clear plastic and synthetic leather with pockets for photos all the way around in which you could display photos of your friends. He talked about building a gondola system in New York for transportation. But although some of my father's products were more successful than others, none of them made the millions he had hoped.

After he left his steady publishing job to become an entrepreneur, there was never enough money to go around, and this was a constant source of conflict between my parents. When I was very young, I remember, we had help around the house: a young babysitter who spoke Spanish, a woman who came in to clean, and an older babysitter, Mrs. Christianson. At that time, we were members of the Bath Club in Lloyd Neck, with its private beach and tennis courts. My sisters took horseback riding lessons and swimming lessons and went to dance classes. At some point, the help around the house, the lessons, and the trips to the Bath Club stopped, because I only remember taking one riding lesson, one ballet lesson, a few piano lessons, and then that was it. There wasn't money for more. I remember my father once becoming furious at me for using too many paper towels to mop up a spill because it was a waste of money. Years later, he showed me a stack of bills from my doctors' visits, as if I were to blame for the devastation of our family's finances.

My father drank, and he had a vicious temper. He would yell at my mother at the slightest provocation, then throw up his hands and walk away. My mother was very quiet during these arguments. She never raised her voice. While he shouted at her, she would look down at the ground as if she were to blame. I remember her standing up for herself only once, holding up a knife.

"Don't come near me," she told him. He didn't.

From an early age, I thought of myself as the peacemaker, the glue that held the family together. At home, there was tension between my parents, tension between my sisters, and tension especially between my sister Robin and my father. Robin was always a little wild. By her early teens, she was already wearing makeup and miniskirts. She started dating a guy from "the wrong side of the tracks." The boy was much older than her, with dark curly hair and a black pickup truck. They would speed off together into town, not coming back until late at night. When my father attempted to ground my sister, she simply ignored him, waltzing out through the front door and never looking back. My father knew he couldn't control Robin, and this enraged him.

Watching my sisters' teenage misadventures made me resolve to always be "the good one." Every time they got into trouble, I quietly promised myself that I would never make the same mistakes.

Once, Robin and my father got into a fight right outside our bedrooms. My father had his hands on Robin's arms, and she was struggling to free herself, kicking and clawing at him while he clung to her, trying to restrain her. I was terrified he was going to hurt her. I remember I raced out of my room and slid my small body between them, then put my arms out on either side of me; I pleaded with them to stop. But I wasn't strong enough to separate them. My father shoved me aside, pushing Robin through the open door of her room, where she fell onto her bed. He crouched over her writhing body, his hands around her neck, yelling at her, shaking her. It occurred to me that he was going to kill her. Somehow Robin wriggled free of him and ran out of the house, along the driveway, and out onto the road. My mother and I got in the car to go look for her. Eventually, we found her, hiding behind tall hedges near our bus stop, crying.

Another time I remember going to look for Robin in the woods beyond our house. She was bleeding. I don't know where the blood came from. In my memory, this moment seems like one from a bad dream, where I don't know exactly what's happening or why.

The police were called to our house more than once because of disturbances. I remember the lights of the patrol cars in the driveway, the crunch of the gravel, doors slamming, then the knock on the door that finally stilled the shouting. When I think back on it now, I wonder who called the police. Our neighbors were too far away to hear anything. Maybe it was me.

CHAPTER 7

Carolyn

In their respective rooms, Grace and Carolyn looked out across a city that was now a grid of familiar addresses for the photography studios and advertising agencies where they went for their shoots. They were both so pragmatic, these girls, so completely determined to win their independence. But that didn't mean they weren't also romantic. Out there somewhere in the city, they knew, a man was waiting for each of them, their perfect match.

Grace had her own gramophone player, so up in her room, they played their favorite records on repeat. *Manhattan Tower* by Gordon Jenkins had come out the year before, an entire album of songs and stories about a young man who comes to New York to live in a Manhattan apartment tower and who falls in love. The music was sweeping and sentimental, interspersed with the sounds of taxi horns and traffic hum, an echo of the world outside the windows of their own tower. Then there was Grace's favorite song, Nat King Cole's *Nature Boy*, just released earlier in the year and still at number one.

At the Barbizon, Carolyn and Grace lay on their sides on Grace's single bed, heads propped on hands, listening to its strange, lulling lyrics over and over. "The greatest thing you'll ever learn," Nat sang, his voice like velvet, "is just to love and be loved in return."

Carolyn had already left a boyfriend back in Steubenville. His name was John Criss, and they'd dated the summer after she graduated high school. John had seen her photo in all the newspapers after she was crowned the town's beauty queen, and he thought she was the most beautiful girl he'd ever seen. So he tracked down her number and called to ask her out; Carolyn was flattered and said yes. John was clean-cut and well dressed, a year older than her and a sophomore at Ohio State. He took Carolyn to the movies in town; they went to the dance hall at Ogilvy Park. A photograph survives of the two of them double-dating with friends, John gazing over at Carolyn, with her blue-black hair and movie-star smile, looking like a man unable to believe his luck. At the end of each evening, John would walk Carolyn back to her house on Pennsylvania Avenue, his hand in hers, but that was as far as it went. Carolyn's stepfather, Joe, would be waiting at the door, making sure John didn't get any farther than the front porch.

John's mother was also concerned about the relationship. She could see that her son was falling in love with Carolyn, and she didn't want him distracted from his studies at Ohio State when he returned in the fall. Mrs. Criss knew that Carolyn hoped to move to New York to model, so she offered to give her extra money to help her leave town. Carolyn took the money. That fall, John returned to Columbus, and Carolyn boarded her train to New York.

Grace's first love was already two years in the past. Harper Davis was a schoolmate of her brother, Kell. Harper had dark eyes and a broad brow beneath wavy black hair. He took Grace to basketball games and dances, and Grace pasted mementos from each of their dates in her scrapbook: the wrapper from the stick of gum Harper gave her on New Year's Eve; the pressed flowers from his bouquets; the business card from the store where he bought her a silvery heart-shaped charm on Valentine's Day. Then, in 1944, Harper graduated and immediately enlisted in the Navy to do his part in the war. Before he left, Grace tearfully called off the relationship. Her father had demanded that she end it; she was too young for a serious love affair. Grace, still the obedient daughter, complied. By the time Harper returned from service, Grace was already packing her bags to leave for New York.

Even at the Barbizon, at a point in their lives where they were focused on career and adventure, the prospect of a husband still hovered somewhere in the near future for Carolyn and Grace, an event on which everything hinged. A good man meant a good life: a nice safe home, a stable and happy existence. Choosing badly would mean suffering the consequences. Grace had a matchmaker's instincts. She had become convinced that Carolyn might be a good match for her older brother. Kell was twenty-two, newly graduated from college, and still single. Up in the rooms at the Barbizon, Grace speculated. What if Carolyn and Kell fell in love and she and Carolyn ended up sisters-in-law?

That summer, Grace engineered a meeting at her family home, on Henry Avenue in East Falls, just outside Philadelphia. Built by Grace's father in the Colonial style, the Kelly mansion was surrounded by grounds and trees, with so many bedrooms and bathrooms that no matter how many times Carolyn counted, she still lost track. That weekend, the Kellys were all assembled, four siblings and two parents, all of them fair-haired, energetic, and able. The mansion, the manicured grounds, the staff, the regimented schedule of the day—all of this allowed houseguests to go from one enjoyable activity to another without having to pause to clean or cook or weed or launder. For Carolyn, the house on Henry Avenue was a stark contrast to her own home, the clapboard house with its pointed gable, its three rooms upstairs and two rooms down, the fractured mix of stepfather and half siblings inside.

At meals and excursions, Grace made sure her brother and Carolyn had chances to spend time together. Carolyn and Kell sat next to each other at breakfast, lunch, and dinner. They walked into town side by side. There was no doubt that Kell was good-looking, with his neat crew cut and strong jaw. But his focus, as it had been since childhood, was on sports. Kell was a champion rower. The summer before, the entire family had traveled to England to see him compete in the Diamond Sculls race at Henley-on-Thames. Kell had won—

and he was still talking about the achievement. It wasn't that Carolyn wasn't impressed; it was just that they had so little in common. Kell was two years older, but even so, he struck her as being too similar to the high school jocks she'd left behind in Steubenville.

Carolyn told Grace. Grace understood, but she was not deterred. She was going to keep her eyes open for someone else.

BACK IN THE CITY, Grace was taking on more modeling jobs, fitting in her assignments around her classes at the Academy. She started lightening her hair to the palest blond. Gone were the sensible shoes, cardigans, and tweed skirts that she used to wear when they'd first arrived at the Barbizon. In their place were cocktail dresses and fur stoles for going out to parties. In the evenings, Grace began leaving behind her horn-rimmed glasses, fearful that if she wore glasses, prospective suitors might fail to notice her. Going without her glasses meant she couldn't see more than a foot ahead of her, but on the upside, it gave her a distant, dreamy look, which men seemed to find irresistible.

That same year, Grace made her first real New York conquest, the film actor Alexander D'Arcy. She had met Alex at a Park Avenue party she'd attended with friends from the Academy. Alex was ten years older, six feet tall, with black hair and a pencil mustache. To a young acting student like Grace, Alex was glamorous in the extreme. He'd appeared in films with Cary Grant and Ginger Rogers; he was a friend of Errol Flynn's. That night, he asked Grace out for dinner. "Call me," she said confidently. "I'm at the Barbizon." And he did call. For their first date, he took her to El Morocco, where she sat next to him on the zebra-print banquette; the owner himself, John Perona, came to sit and chat with them at their table. For their second date, they went dancing at the Stork Club under the midnight-blue ceiling filled with winking stars.

With Alex on her arm, Grace's social life was transformed. She wanted Carolyn to join her. Although she had failed to pair Carolyn with her brother, Kell, she had a new idea. Grace had first run into Malcolm Reybold on Long Island, playing tennis on Sherman Fairchild's courts. Sherman was famous for his extravagant parties, which usually lasted the entire weekend. Malcolm was one of Sherman's closest friends. He was older and divorced, but charming and an excellent tennis player. He and Grace had seen each other around town a few times since Long Island.

If Carolyn was interested, Grace would invite Malcolm on a double date.

The four met at the Hawaiian Room, the basement supper club at the Lexington Hotel. The hostess immediately gave Carolyn a string of paper flowers to wear around her neck, which made Carolyn feel less shy, as if she were at a costume party. Malcolm was courteous from the minute they arrived—helping Carolyn with her coat, ushering her ahead of him, holding the door, pulling out her chair. Yes, he was older, but he was also handsome, tall, and broad shouldered, with reddish blond hair. And he was confident.

A band was playing hula music as dancers sashayed in grass skirts. There were beach scenes painted on the walls and tropical palms in giant planters. Carolyn had never eaten Hawaiian food before. She was dazzled by all the unfamiliar names on the menu. Malcolm took matters into his own hands, ordering her "the best thing in the house." Over dinner, he told her stories about his family in Georgia, about his job on Madison Avenue, working for an advertising agency. He laughed easily and often—and made her laugh, too.

Once dinner was over, he led her out onto the dance floor, spinning her away from him, then pulling her back again with perfect ease, as if to let her know that, with him, she was in capable hands.

NOW THAT CAROLYN and Grace had dates to squire them around town, their evenings were transformed. By the time the sun went down, they had pinched their tiny waists into satin cocktail dresses, thrown little fur stoles around their shoulders, and taken the elevator down to the lobby to meet their men. Stepping out onto Sixty-third Street—heels clacking smartly on the sidewalk—they were no longer two girls alone in the city but young women of the world. Where should they go? The answer was anywhere now. In 1948, as a woman without a date, it was impossible to gain entry to the best nightclubs—the club owners didn't want angry wives sneaking in,

surprising cheating husbands out on the town with mistresses. But now that Grace and Carolyn had men on their arms, there was no limit to where they might go. Maybe they'd have dinner at the Stork Club, where the owner always invited them back to lunch the next day, plying them with gifts of Chanel No. 5 and little golden cigarette cases. After dinner they might head over to El Morocco for dancing. Copacabana was best for nightclub shows—and Chinese food. You never knew who you might see there: Frank Sinatra, Ava Gardner, Cary Grant.

Carolyn kept her eyes trained on Grace, who seemed to have a sixth sense for knowing exactly what to do in any situation. She seemed to understand the codes of New York nightlife instinctively, always wearing the right dress, picking up the right fork at the table setting, turning to say the right thing at the right moment. By watching Grace and following her lead, Carolyn learned to maneuver in a world that was completely foreign to her and as far from Steubenville as she could imagine. A little before eleven, Grace and Carolyn would make their excuses, racing outside, two Cinderellas with curfews, arms waving to find a cab to take them back to the Barbizon before the clock struck the hour, always arriving back at the hotel as late as possible but just early enough to avoid a lecture from Mrs. Sibley. They were working models, after all; they knew they had to look fresh in the morning. Besides, there was always the next date, the next evening.

Before long, Alex left for an acting job in Paris, at which point Grace's relationship with him came to its natural conclusion. They had never been serious, after all. But Malcolm and Carolyn were another matter. It didn't matter to Carolyn that Malcolm had already been married, that he had a daughter from that marriage, that he was twelve years older. Malcolm was old-fashioned; he was a gentleman.

He didn't rush Carolyn. He simply wanted to spend time with her. And Carolyn found that if she looked in her heart, she wanted to spend more time with him.

Before 1948 was over, Carolyn found herself packing her bags and leaving town. Eileen Ford had booked her for a six-week shoot for the Sears, Roebuck catalog at the Bill Becker studio in Tucson, Arizona. Although Carolyn would miss the Barbizon, Grace, and, of course, Malcolm, the money was good, and the job would mean excellent visibility: there was hardly a household in America that didn't receive a Sears, Roebuck catalog in the mail. Almost a year after she'd left Ohio to move to New York, Carolyn arrived at the new Idlewild airport in Queens, suitcase in hand, ready to board her first flight. Ten other girls from the Ford agency were going with her.

Eileen had briefed all the girls about Bill Becker, the owner of the largest photographic studio in the country. Eileen had worked for Becker in New York before she founded her agency, coordinating his shoots, packing and shipping the clothes that were going to be photographed out west, and booking the models to be flown there. She knew him well.

"He's a bear," Eileen warned her girls. "He'll try to insult you and embarrass you. Stand your ground."

Becker had his headquarters in Manhattan, but when winter came around, he defected to Tucson, a town with more hours of sunshine than any other city in the United States and where he could shoot for fifteen hours a day.

After Eileen's girls arrived in Tucson, they made straight for the Pioneer Hotel, where they would be staying for the next six weeks. Becker's studio was just outside the city in Tanque Verde. The studio was vast, with a special stage built on a turntable, like a giant

lazy Susan, with a white background behind and a large skylight overhead. As the sun moved in the sky, Bill's assistants would spin the stage to catch the optimal light. It was so hot under the skylight that most of the time the girls were close to fainting. They were all wearing black suede heels, which would get so hot that they would take turns holding a piece of white cardboard over the shoes in an effort to cool them down.

Days were long. Becker had them working from early morning until sundown. Boxes filled with fashions for next spring had been shipped from New York, and the girls dutifully worked their way through every blouse and skirt, jacket and hat, as Becker barked his orders.

At night, after work was done, the girls went back to their hotel and got dressed again, this time for dinner. In their silk and satin cocktail dresses and long gloves, they made their way downstairs to the hotel dining room. Not long after they arrived in Tucson, Carolyn noticed a new guest at the hotel. He was leaning on his elbows against the main fireplace in the lobby, watching her come down the stairs via her reflection in the mirror above the mantel. She recognized him right away—he was Howard Hughes, the film director. Hughes was unmistakable from the magazines, tall and gangling, his black hair slicked back on his head. Carolyn caught his eye in the mirror. Hughes gestured to her to come over, and over she went.

He looked her up and down.

"Are you one of the models?" he wanted to know.

Carolyn nodded.

"Where you from?"

She told him.

It turned out Hughes was in Tucson scouting for talent. He'd just paid close to 9 million dollars for RKO Studios, and he was looking to sign new starlets to his books.

"What would you say if I told you I wanted you to come to Hollywood for a screen test?" he asked.

Carolyn paused.

She warned Hughes that she didn't have any training as an actress.

He told her that if she wanted to take a screen test, he'd arrange for acting classes as part of the deal.

Carolyn thought, *Why not?*

The next day, after shooting was over, she found herself at the Tucson airfield, clutching her overnight bag, the sole passenger aboard one of Hughes's private airplanes en route to Los Angeles. Hughes had a reputation for scheduling meetings at unconventional hours, and by the time Carolyn landed in L.A. and the driver dropped her at the RKO lot, it was very late at night. The driver told her to walk to the back of the building ahead; tentatively, she stepped into what looked like an aircraft hangar. Ahead of her, she could see a series of storage areas, with sets and props leaning against the walls. Her chest was tight with nerves, and it occurred to her to go back and get in the car again. Instead, she kept walking until she reached a door at the very back of the hanger.

Carolyn took a breath, knocked on the door, and waited. She heard a voice telling her to come in. She cracked the door. On the other side, there was Hughes, sitting with his feet up on a giant desk. He was wearing a striped knit sailor top and long duck pants, with scuffed boat shoes, as if he'd just come in from sailing. Carolyn stood quietly in the middle of the room while Hughes looked her up and down again, appraising her silently with stealthy eyes. Behind him, there was a life-sized picture of the actress Jane Russell, in the movie *The Outlaw*, directed by Hughes during the war. Russell's breasts were barely covered in a peasant blouse that had fallen seductively from her shoulder.

Finally, Hughes spoke up.

"Pull your bangs over to one side," he told Carolyn. "I want to see your forehead."

Carolyn did as she was told.

"We will do the screen test tomorrow," Hughes said.

Carolyn thought for a moment. Then she took a deep breath and told Hughes that no, she didn't think she wanted to do the test after all. She turned around and ran back out the door, through the maze of sets and props, until finally she was out on the lot again and free, her heart pounding in her ears. Carolyn knew the signs. She had grown up with a stepfather who leered at her that way. She knew a threat when she saw one.

In the future, she decided, she would leave the acting to Grace.

WHEN THE SHOOT in Tucson was finally over, Carolyn returned to New York with relief. It was blessedly cold in New York and comforting to be back at the hotel, with Mrs. Sibley behind her usual counter and Oscar ready to tip his hat whenever she came and went. Although Carolyn had been given a new room, on another floor, the green bedspread on her twin bed was the same, the curtains identical to the ones in the room she had left behind. In its own way, the hotel felt like home. She also returned to Malcolm. In a short period of time, it had become hard for Carolyn to imagine New York without her new beau, as if Manhattan had suddenly switched to Technicolor and there was no going back to black-and-white. Malcolm was so attentive, so kind. He always knew exactly where to go and what to order once they got there. He loved good food and wine, friendship, conversation. "Never stop laughing or loving" was his motto, and he lived by it.

What's more, Malcolm took care of her—and this made Carolyn

feel safe. Ever since childhood she had known that her looks had singled her out for male attention, and while the way she looked might have been her salvation, it also put her at risk. When she worked at the department store in Steubenville, there had been an older man who used to come in and buy clothing for his daughter. Everyone called him "Jimmy the Greek," and even though Carolyn had given him no encouragement, Jimmy had fallen in love with her. Each day he came into the store, watching her from a distance, following her back home to Pennsylvania Avenue once her shift was over. For a while, it seemed there was no way to get away from Jimmy. Even now, a year after she'd left Ohio, Jimmy had tracked her down, driving to New York and leaving gifts for her at the desk at the Barbizon. Jimmy was a gambler, and he had clearly gotten lucky, because the gifts included some very expensive jewelry. When Malcolm learned about Jimmy the Greek, he helped Carolyn rewrap the gifts, and together they delivered them back to Jimmy's hotel. Whenever Malcolm told the story at parties, Carolyn laughed along—it was all a great joke. But what made her happiest was the message behind the story: she belonged to Malcolm now.

CHAPTER 8

Nina

I never met Grace as a child, although I'm told she did visit when I was a baby. What I do remember are the letters to my mother, which arrived every month or so, in thick creamy envelopes, stamped with the red-and-gold royal seal of Monaco. My mother would write back right away, long letters that she mailed from the post office when she went into town to buy groceries. Somewhere along the way, the letters were lost—along with so many of my mother's possessions.

Then there were Grace's movies. Whenever one was showing on TV, my mother and I made sure we watched it together. *To Catch a Thief* gave me my first glimpses of Monaco, the place where I knew Grace lived, and where my mother had been the bridesmaid, with its hot blue skies, red roofs, and roads looping up into the hillsides. I loved all the Hitchcock films, but especially *Rear Window*, the way Grace first swept into the frame, her beautiful features blurred but coming into focus as Jimmy Stewart opens his eyes, her clothes, each dress more beautiful than the next. My favorite of all Grace's films was *High Society*, where she played Tracy Lord, the society girl about to be married. My mother always told me that the ring Grace wore in the film was her *actual* engagement ring, given to her by Prince Rainier, and that *High Society* was Grace's last film. After shooting was over, Grace moved to Monaco and gave up acting forever.

Apart from the films and the letters, though, it was very hard for me to connect Grace with my mother. Growing up, my mother hardly ever spoke of the past, so it's only in retrospect that I've been able to understand that she *did* show me glimpses of her former life with Grace; she just didn't tell me she was doing it.

AT LEAST TWO or three times a year, I would go with my mother into the city to the ballet, never realizing how important dance had been to her and to Grace when they were younger.

We always drove into the city. I think my mother felt like she couldn't risk rousing suspicions by taking the train; she didn't want people wondering why a young girl of my age wasn't in school in the middle of a weekday. I can picture her behind the wheel, the window just open, smoke from her cigarette trailing out behind us, me wearing one of my party dresses handed down to me from my sisters. In the city, we saw matinees of *Les Sylphides, Sleeping Beauty, Petrushka, Giselle,* and *Coppélia.* We went to *Swan Lake* more than once. My mother loved these ballets, their spellbound heroines: Odette in *Swan Lake*, trapped and unable to escape, or Giselle, driven to death by a broken heart, who rises to save her lover from evil spirits before returning to her grave. Usually we'd have seats in the orchestra, close to the stage, about six rows back, and when I looked over at my mother, her face would be lit by the glow from the stage lights, tears running down her cheeks.

The Nutcracker was my favorite. Balanchine's new production of the ballet had just moved to the new State Theater at Lincoln Center, and my mother made sure we had tickets each November, right after Thanksgiving. My favorite part came at the end of act 1, when Marie and the Little Prince turn their backs to the audience and walk together toward the forest of fir trees as the snow drifts magically from the sky.

After the performance was over, my mother would take me by the hand and we'd walk together along Broadway until we reached the Automat at Fifty-seventh Street. I loved the Automat, the way the food was kept in little gleaming glass boxes along the walls. We'd go straight to the cashier and change dollar bills for nickels; then I'd walk up and down the length of the restaurant, making my selections. If I couldn't reach the box I wanted, my mother would lift me up at the waist, and I'd drop my coins in the slot, winding the knob until the sandwich or slice of pie appeared behind the glass door, like a prize waiting to be claimed. We ate slowly, making each mouthful last, never in any hurry to leave and return home.

My mother never told me that the Automat was the place where the photographer had discovered her back in her Barbizon days. She never told me she took dance classes as a young woman or that she had gone to see Balanchine's dancers with Grace. Instead, she shared with me these things that she had always enjoyed, and was happy when I enjoyed them, too.

When I was nine, we made a special trip to see *The Nutcracker* with Suzanne Farrell dancing the Sugar Plum Fairy. Somehow, my mother had a connection to Suzanne: it may have been that they'd met at a dance event, or through Grace, who was a patron of the ballet in Monaco. After the performance was over, my mother and I waited at the stage door until Suzanne and her husband, the dancer Paul Mejia, came out to meet us. Suzanne invited us back to their apartment, in a high-rise building not far from the theater. I was so starstruck. Suzanne was beautiful, gracious, and kind. She was originally from Ohio, like my mother. I remember sitting on her bed as she looked through her closet for something to give to me. "Would you like this?" she asked, showing me a navy woolen coat she no longer needed. I was only nine, but I was tall for my age, and Suzanne was so petite that the coat fit me perfectly. I wore that coat for as long as I could, until the sleeves reached to my elbows. The year following our meeting, Suzanne left the New York City Ballet after a falling-out with Balanchine.

We never saw Suzanne again, but there were more trips to the ballet, and I loved every one of them. When we got back to the house on Long Island, my mother always put one of her Tchaikovsky records on the sound system in the living room, and I'd whirl around, impersonating the ballerinas I'd seen at the theater, the gorgeous sounds of the orchestra filling the room up to the rafters.

Then, whenever *The Red Shoes* played on television, we made sure to watch. It was one of my mother's favorite movies. In the film, Moira Shearer plays Vicky, a prima ballerina who has the starring role in a ballet based on the Hans Christian Andersen fairy tale "The Red Shoes." Early in the story, Vicky falls in love with a young composer, but finds herself torn between her love for him and her devotion to the ballet impresario Lermontov. Forced to choose between her lover and her dancing—and knowing she can't have both—Vicky eventually breaks down. Before a performance in Monte Carlo, she dances out into the streets, spinning uncontrollably, unable to stop, as if bewitched by her shoes like the girl in the fairy tale, until she jumps or maybe falls in front of a passing train.

The film ends with Vicky lying close to death on a stretcher. Her legs are broken and bloody—she will never dance again. She asks her lover to remove the red shoes.

This was life's tragedy, the film seemed to say: that art and love were incompatible, for a woman at least. I remember the tears in my mother's eyes as she watched.

At the time, I thought my mother loved *The Red Shoes* for the same reasons I did—the gorgeous colors of the costumes and Vicky's red hair, the dance sequences that looked like vanishing dreams. But in hindsight, I've come to believe there was another reason she felt such a strong attachment to Vicky's story and to the ballet in general. I think she understood the stories viscerally. Out on Long Island, she, too, was held captive by her life's circumstances, caught in a spell cast long ago, without any way to break it.

CHAPTER 9

Carolyn

Like so much of my parents' marriage, their wedding day remains something of a mystery to me. When I was a child, no one ever talked about the ceremony or reception. The anniversary was never celebrated. While I could go to my mother's closet and find the bridesmaid's dress from Grace's wedding in Monaco, I never saw her own wedding outfit—she had given it away to her cousin. Many years later, when I started to look into my mother's story, I had to hire a researcher in Florida to go to the city clerk's office to track down their marriage certificate in order to even know the date of the wedding: Monday, March 14, 1949.

My parents were married at the First Presbyterian Church in Miami Beach. A local newspaper report explains that Malcolm's cousin and his wife served as witnesses; they lived nearby. After the short ceremony, the couple went to the North Shore Hotel for the reception.

Most women chose to have a maid of honor or a bridesmaid or

two to stand alongside them on such a day. But Grace was busy in New York appearing in her graduation play, *The Philadelphia Story*, so Carolyn was completely alone, stepping into her new life without a friend by her side.

Only one photograph from the wedding survives. In it, Carolyn and Malcolm are carefully making the first cut in a small, three-layered wedding cake. Malcolm's hand is resting on Carolyn's as she holds the knife. With a model's professionalism, my mother has wrapped her other hand gently around his arm, so that her new wedding band can be seen. She's wearing a pale tailored suit, with a jacket that buttons up to the neck, and a straight skirt that falls to midcalf. Malcolm wears a gray business suit, with a tie and boutonniere. Carolyn looks calm and tender; Malcolm is the only one smiling. When the celebrations were over—and the wedding night survived—the couple took a honeymoon trip, first stopping in Palm Beach and then at Sea Island, just off the coast of Georgia. After a week, they drove back to New York to start their life together. Carolyn had already packed up her belongings at the Barbizon so she could go directly to her new home—Malcolm's apartment on the East Side in Tudor City.

Grace was also packing her bags and leaving the Barbizon, but for a very different reason.

Earlier in the year, she had started seeing someone new: Don Richardson, her acting professor in her final year at the Academy. Like Malcolm, Don was an older man, recently divorced. Don lived in a small and sparsely furnished apartment in an old unheated brownstone on Thirty-third Street. With Don, Grace saw a very different side of New York from the one she had experienced with Alex. Don was a professional actor and theater director. He didn't care about nightclubs or money; he was an artist, living for his craft, a bohemian. When Grace went to visit him on Thirty-Third, she would have to help him collect firewood from old packing cases left in the street by the local rug dealers, so that Don could light a fire to keep her warm.

Initially, she kept her relationship with Don secret, not only from others at the Academy—they likely would have been shocked that she was dating a member of the faculty—but also from her parents. While Carolyn was away, though, Grace decided to take Don home to meet her family. Grace knew that her parents would most likely disapprove of her new boyfriend but was hopeful that Don could still win them over. If they just gave him a chance, she reasoned, they might discover they loved him just as much as she did.

For Grace's Catholic family, however, Don was instantly unsuitable. There were three strikes against him in their eyes: he was older, divorced, and Jewish. The visit did not go well. By the time the weekend was over, Jack Kelly had told Grace to end the relationship and move back to Philadelphia. "I cried so much," Grace wrote in a letter to a friend after the weekend was over. "Hell just can't be much worse than what I went through." Grace was permitted to return to Manhattan for the day, to clear out her room at the Barbizon and bring home her belongings, but essentially she was forbidden to return to New York for the foreseeable future. For better or worse, Grace's family had intervened in a relationship with a man they found unacceptable.

Carolyn had no such protection.

Now THAT SHE was married, Carolyn set aside her own interests and happily focused on those of her husband. Back then, Carolyn was at the height of her success—making far more money as a model than Malcolm was in his advertising job—and the couple could afford to live well. Malcolm wasn't interested in the ballet, so Carolyn no longer went to City Center each week to see Balanchine's dancers. Her new husband preferred to eat at expensive restaurants and go to fashionable nightclubs, so Carolyn stopped going to the Automat for her lunches. Malcolm loved tennis, so she tried to take up the game, but she couldn't keep up with him. On Friday evenings, the new Mrs. Reybold climbed into the cream-colored Buick Roadmaster convertible that Malcolm had bought her as a wedding gift. Malcolm drove, and she snuggled next to him on the bench seat, wearing sunglasses with a silk scarf wrapped around her hair. The car was just as elegant and modern as the good-looking couple behind the wheel. Malcolm had married his ideal girl—gorgeous, lively, successful, social.

They were headed for Long Island and Sherman Fairchild's castle, Eastfair, on the edge of the Long Island Sound. At Eastfair, days were long and romantic, spent sunbathing by the pool (for Carolyn) or playing tennis on the clay courts (for Malcolm). There were cocktails and intimate dinner parties in the evenings, everyone gathering in the living room with its two grand pianos, a wide fireplace, and high ceilings. Fellow guests included actors and actresses, fashion models who had come to Eastfair to work on their portfolios at Sherman's photography studio, and jazz musicians who recorded in the castle's recording studio by day and entertained the guests by night. Photographs from that summer show Carolyn and Malcolm very much in love, Carolyn smiling over at her new husband on a friend's boat, or Malcolm wrapping her in his arms in a movie-star clinch.

For Grace—still grounded in Philadelphia—Carolyn had achieved a kind of ultimate freedom. As a wife, Carolyn could go

anywhere she pleased. Meanwhile, Grace's parents remained determined to prevent a reunion between their daughter and Don Richardson: after the disaster of the Barbizon, Jack and Margaret Kelly weren't taking any risks. When Grace won a part in summer stock in New Hope, thirty-five miles away, Mr. and Mrs. Kelly made her drive there and back each day rather than find lodging of her own nearby. It was while performing in New Hope, however, that Grace heard she'd been cast in a new production of Strindberg's *The Father.* The play was opening in Boston before transferring to Broadway in November. Grace's parents could hardly expect her to drive back and forth to Boston and New York each day during the run of the show. Finally, Grace wore the Kellys down. They were forced to let her go.

On opening night on Broadway in November, both Carolyn and Malcolm were in the audience. "When Grace first walked out onstage, she looked so fresh and pretty and breathtaking," Carolyn later remembered. "I think that's when I first realized she was going to be *someone*." Grace played Bertha, a young woman whose parents are unable to agree on her future. The mother wants Bertha to stay at home and become an artist; the father wants her to move into town so she can study to be a teacher. As fighting between the parents escalates, Bertha becomes increasingly bewildered and heartbroken. In the role of a daughter with excessively controlling parents, Grace could draw on her own experience.

Although Grace received good reviews in the press, the play failed to capture the imagination of theatergoers. It closed in early February 1950, after only sixty-nine performances. For the first time since she had graduated from the Academy, Grace was out of work. She was single, living with her parents, and not at all happy about it. Malcolm and Carolyn decided to do something to lift Grace's spirits. They invited her on a weekend road trip to Canada in the new Buick. Malcolm's plan was to return the favor and play matchmaker for Grace. He invited his friend Jack Duff along for the ride. Jack had a reputation as one of New York's most eligible bachelors; he was also a member of the exclusive Seigniory Club, in Quebec, where the four friends were planning to stay on their weekend away.

The group arrived at the Seigniory in time for dinner. In the morning, they woke to views across the Ottawa River and mountains frosted with snow as bright as wedding cakes. That weekend they skated on the frozen lake and hiked in snowshoes into the hills. Grace and Carolyn also ventured out together for an afternoon drive, leaving the men behind, so they could have time together to talk. Grace informed Carolyn that she had no interest in Jack, and Carolyn understood.

That same afternoon, Carolyn realized that she had forgotten to affix the new car registration to the window, so she asked Grace to look for it in the glove compartment. Grace handed the registration to Carolyn, who noticed that Malcolm's license was pinned to the back. This was how Carolyn discovered that her new husband had lied to her about his age. He had told her he was thirty-two. In fact, Malcolm Durbec Reybold had been born on February 25, 1910. It wasn't difficult for Carolyn to do the math. Her own mother had been born that year. That meant he was nearly forty, the same age as her mother.

Grace and Carolyn drove back to the lodge, where Grace urged Carolyn to confront her husband. They found Malcolm at the bar and asked him to explain the license and the birth date. Malcolm didn't flinch as Carolyn explained how hurt and betrayed she felt. Instead, he laughed loudly, slapping her on the back and claiming it had all been a great joke. For the rest of the weekend, he made a point of bringing up the license often, laughing again at Carolyn's foolishness in taking him seriously.

After they left Canada, Carolyn tried to put the subject of Malcolm's age aside. Perhaps her new husband was right. Maybe it was just a joke, nothing important in the greater scheme of things. Besides, she was too busy—and too happy—to dwell on it much. Work was going so well. For the next year, she appeared each month in *Mademoiselle's* "Scoops of the Month" feature, as "Joan," the magazine's quintessential reader. In the coming months, she traveled to Washington, D.C., to Princeton, and to Puerto Rico for her new job. For the magazine's Christmas issue of 1950, she stood in a window at Lord & Taylor's department store posed beside a mannequin. By now, she was completely at ease in front of the camera, radiating a kind of effortless joy. The editors at the magazine took note: marriage agreed with Carolyn.

Grace had still not been cast in another Broadway show, but

she was faring better going up for parts in plays being staged for the new medium of television. It turned out that Grace had the kind of subtlety and looks that played well on camera. In 1950, she appeared in eleven televised plays, shuttling back and forth from Philadelphia to New York for rehearsals and shoots. Meanwhile, a producer at 20th Century Fox had seen Grace in *The Father* and invited her to audition for a tiny role in the movie *Fourteen Hours*. She won the part and accepted, but all the travel between New York and Philadelphia was wearing on her nerves. Reluctantly, her parents finally agreed she could rent an apartment of her own in the city. In October of 1950, Grace moved into the Manhattan House, a sleek new building on East Sixty-sixth Street that her father had helped to construct, providing the gleaming white bricks for the exterior. Mr. and Mrs. Kelly demanded that Grace find a roommate, so she asked a friend from the Academy, Sally Parrish, to move in with her.

Although it wasn't easy to gain entry to the Manhattan House— references were required, and family background was taken into account—Grace informed the management company that when the final apartments became available in the New Year, she would like to put in a good word for her friends the Reybolds.

Malcolm and Carolyn were going to need an extra bedroom: Carolyn was pregnant. Grace had been among the first to know. The baby was due in June 1951. Malcolm was the proud husband; Carolyn was glowing. She had always loved children and had a special affection for them. Growing up, her half brother and sister were so much younger that she babysat them often, wiping their little faces and tending to their scrapes and bruises with a mother's care. Pregnancy felt like a fulfillment of purpose, the tiny fluttering of the baby inside her a prediction of future joy. Since the wedding, they had been living in Malcolm's bachelor apartment overlooking the construction site of the new United Nations building. It wasn't nearly big enough for a family, and Carolyn was grateful that Grace stepped in to help them find the apartment at the Manhattan House.

In the new year, Carolyn and Malcolm moved into their new home on the eighteenth floor, with Grace downstairs on the ninth. The Reybolds' apartment had views looking out across the city from wide, long windows. Malcolm picked out the furnishings, all of them custom made and in the latest modern style. The walls of the living room were painted a daring azure blue, offset by an accent wall covered in plaid wallpaper and a plush beige carpet. The couch was striped in blue, pink, and orange sateen. There was a tall rust-colored easy chair for Malcolm, sleek mahogany wood furniture, and rows of shelves to house his collection of books. The master bathroom was tiled in white, with deep red walls and towels monogrammed R in a matching red. Their neighbors at the Manhattan House were a young and accomplished crowd: architects, advertising and television executives, journalists, musicians, and actors.

Manhattan House was being written about in the newspapers and nominated for architecture awards, considered ahead of its time. Malcolm—who coveted all that was modern and fashionable—took enormous pride in their new living arrangements.

In the mornings, Carolyn kissed her husband good-bye, and he strode out of the building and along Sixty-sixth Street, walking to his offices at J. Walter Thompson on Madison Avenue; his suits, ties, and shirts kept beautifully pressed by the couple's new housekeeper, under Carolyn's clever supervision. Now that she had begun to show, she began to phase out her modeling jobs. That June, she appeared in *Seventeen,* modeling matching scarlet lipstick and nails, shown only from the shoulders up. Soon after that, Eileen took her off the books at the agency, at least until she got her waist back.

In her current state, going out to parties and restaurants simply wasn't done. There were no more weekends at Sherman's, no evenings at the Stork Club or the Colony. When Malcolm went out, he went alone or with his work colleagues and clients. Like all women of a certain class and income, Carolyn knew a proper pregnancy should be a discreet affair, kept between a husband and wife and close family and friends, not something in which the outside world should share. Usually so stylish, Carolyn bought herself comfortable wrap dresses, smocks, and shirtwaists to wear at home. In her confinement, she began decorating the baby's nursery, picking out the crib, the curtains, the rugs, and the dresser with elaborate care. Often alone in the evenings now, she stood in the living room of the Manhattan House, looking across the glittering towers of the city, in her nest in the sky.

Grace's new apartment was downstairs, number 9A. It had parquet floors, its own terrace, and a wood-burning fireplace, with long windows overlooking the private landscaped courtyard in the center of the complex. Everything about the apartment was modern and new, but as if to counteract its glamour, Grace's mother had furnished it on Grace's behalf, and the resulting decor was awash in shades of brown, filled with bland and practical family furniture shipped from Philadelphia. It didn't matter to Grace. She was back in New York. It was as if her Barbizon days had been restored, this time without the curfew.

Grace's apartment became the hub of their social lives. In the middle of the living room sat a large round black Formica table, which doubled for dinner and drinks: you could swivel it up for food and then down again for coffee or cocktails. Grace cooked for her friends, serving up hearty meat-and-potato dishes, with home-baked lemon pie for dessert. Carolyn often joined these gatherings, either alone or with Malcolm. She was grateful that despite her swelling figure, she could still see friends at Grace's. After dinner, there were jokes and confidences, charades, and their favorite activity, fortune-telling.

It was Malcolm who had introduced the group to astrology, and the Manhattan House friends quickly adopted horoscopes as a kind of faith. Malcolm had given them a book, *The Pursuit of Destiny*, written by an occultist by the name of Muriel Bruce Hasbrouck. Like other astrologers, Hasbrouck believed that the movement of the planets and human fate were intimately connected, but hers was a new approach. Instead of assigning twelve astrological signs by birth date as other astrologers did, she divided the year into ten-day cycles, each of them represented by a card in the tarot pack. To read your fortune, you found the ten-day cycle that included your birthday, then read the description that followed.

Born on November 12, Grace was a Six of Scorpio. Her tarot card was the nine of cups, representing "Pleasure." According to the book, she was possessed with "magnetic charm, showmanship, creative imagination and staying power." People born under the sign of Six of Scorpio, the author wrote, "take center of any stage, as by divine right, and occupy it successfully with popularity and charm." For Grace, still a struggling actress, this was comforting, confirmation she was on the right track. But although Six of Scorpios "contain the greatest creative power, they are also capable of the most compelling harm." On the negative side, Six of Scorpios are prone to disregard the feelings and sufferings of others. "Their one desire is to succeed, to gain possession of what they want, or to get their own way by imposing their will on other people, and this desire is so strong that it outweighs everything else, especially kindness or justice."

In order to achieve happiness in life, the book advised, it was important to keep both negative and positive elements in the correct balance.

Carolyn was born on August 19 and was a Seven of Leo. Her tarot card was the seven of wands, representing "Valor." People born under this sign have "courage and resourcefulness, imagination and intensity." This was absolutely true of Carolyn, who had come to New York alone, with nothing more than two suitcases and her wits. But Seven of Leos, the book explained, struggle with a central conflict, namely their desire to succeed and their tendency to "scatter their energies so widely that the effort to concentrate on a number of things at the same time destroys their mental balance, making them highly irritable, nervous and undependable."

Malcolm was born on February 25, so his sign was Eight of Pisces. His positive qualities were his "constructive intelligence, compassionate intensity and practical executive ability," a description that he loved. On the negative side, the book explained, those born under Eight of Pisces can be "intolerant and narrow minded, self-righteous, and unfriendly . . . ultra-critical of other people's ideas, behavior and actions . . . . When negative, their human sympathy turns destructive, taking the form of cruelty and bitterness toward people who do not conform to their rigid standards." Malcolm's tarot card was the eight of cups, "Abandoned Success."

Grace and Carolyn revisited the pages of *The Pursuit of Destiny* often, searching for new insights and explanations. Grace was still only twenty-one; Carolyn, twenty-two. The larger part of their lives lay ahead, not behind; their characters were still only half formed. Grace was at the beginning of her career—she'd just made her first film, *Fourteen Hours*, appearing on-screen for about two minutes in an uncredited role. Carolyn was about to become a mother for the first time. How would her marriage and life change? Could she keep her career? For both young women, on the cusp of everything, the notion that the planets were in control—that character was innate and waiting to be revealed—offered a kind of consoling reassurance.

CAROLYN'S FIRST CHILD was born via C-section on June 19, 1951, after a labor that stalled for too long. Malcolm chose the name Deborah Jill. Carolyn brought their new daughter home to Manhattan House the following week. Carolyn only had one person in mind for godmother, and when she asked Grace to guide Jill and take care of her spiritually, Grace immediately said yes.

That first summer with the baby, Carolyn found herself absorbed in the small duties of being a new mother, the urgently compelling but rarely recorded moments that make up a new parent's day: the cries from the nursery in the morning that sent Carolyn hurrying to Jill's crib, the bottles to be made and rinsed, all the tiny outfits to be neatly folded and put away. Then there were the walks over to Central Park in the hazy late afternoons of July and August, with the baby in her shiny new carriage, a white cotton cap on her head. In those first few months, Jill passed her earliest milestones, the first smile, the first cold, the first tooth.

As the baby grew, Carolyn found herself reshaped. She no longer saw the world from her own solitary perspective; now it was refracted through the experience of her daughter. There was no doubt that little Jill would grow up in a home that was financially stable—Malcolm's career in advertising was going so well—but even so, Carolyn kept one eye on the family bank account those first few months. Her husband liked to live well; they were going to miss her income. Eileen Ford made it clear that the doors were open whenever Carolyn was ready to come back; Eileen herself had quickly returned to work after the births of both her children. Carolyn knew she was lucky in this respect: while most employers in 1951 told their pregnant employees to leave and never come back, Eileen actively encouraged her girls to return to work after having children—as long as they had shed their baby weight, of course.

So in the new year of 1952, six months after giving birth, Carolyn left little Jill with her nanny and made the short walk over to Second Avenue and the Ford offices. Here, Eileen took out her tape measure, wrapped it once around Carolyn's waist, and declared her back to form. Soon after, Eileen decided she was ready to promote Carolyn from a "junior" to a "miss." While "juniors" worked exclusively for the teenage market, "misses" appealed to slightly older customers as well: brides-to-be, newlyweds, and young mothers. By

June, Carolyn was on the cover of *Family Circle* magazine wearing a pale pink taffeta wedding gown, complete with crown and veil, holding up a spray of roses and with a large diamond engagement ring on her finger. That same summer, she posed as a "young modern newlywed" next to a white-jacketed husband to advertise tablecloths: "When all eyes are on *their* table they make sure it's at its very best."

It felt natural to be back in front of the camera. Carolyn knew how to widen her eyes to keep them looking bright, to turn her head to show her most appealing profile, to hold her back straight and her shoulders square while she angled an arm or leg this way and that. In the magazines, Carolyn played the ideal of the modern woman—smiling, polished, self-assured, married or about to be married, awash in postwar prosperity, with every appliance and product at her disposal. When she ran back home at the end of the day to baby Jill, she felt that she was doing her part to fulfill the fantasies she promoted in those photographs. She was doing her duty, keeping the baby neat and smiling, the apartment organized, and her husband happy.

CAROLYN STAYED CLOSE to Manhattan House, but Grace was its satellite, in almost constant motion. Her movie career was taking off, and she was traveling all the time. She made *High Noon* in California opposite Gary Cooper, then *Mogambo* in Africa and England with John Ford. From there she was called back to Hollywood for her first film with Alfred Hitchcock, *Dial M for Murder*, closely followed by *Rear Window*. Although she had signed a contract with MGM, she made it a condition that she would be able to live in New York when she wasn't filming, so when each shoot came to a close, she returned to the Manhattan House and her "family" there: Carolyn, Malcolm, and Jill. Then, in the spring of 1953, Carolyn announced she was pregnant again, and that October, she gave birth to another daughter, Robin Brooke Reybold.

Malcolm picked out the name, as he had done with Jill. After enduring another C-section, Carolyn was pale, but it was nothing

❖

that a daily swipe of red lipstick wouldn't fix. Grace took the elevator upstairs to the eighteenth floor to visit whenever she could, spoiling little Jill as she adjusted to having a new sister. By now, Jill had grown into a toddler with a mop of light brown hair curling around her ears and eyes that had turned to deep brown, just like her mother's.

Robin was just a few months old when Carolyn returned to modeling. The family needed the extra income more than ever. Malcolm had been flying home from a business trip when he began spitting blood. Plagued by ulcers for many years, Malcolm was suffering from complications, and they were severe. The doctors removed three-quarters of his stomach, some of his upper intestine, and part of his pancreas. It would be many months before he would be able to work again. The medical bills were piling up, and someone needed to pay the rent.

After weeks of trying out for jobs and failing to win a single one, Carolyn finally secured a booking for the May issue of *Seventeen*. After that, she didn't appear in another magazine until July. The months crawled by, with Carolyn going up for job after job. By the time 1954 was over, she had appeared in only one small feature and a mere five advertising campaigns. Eileen Ford did her best to drum up more work, but the reality was that Carolyn's greatest success had been in magazines for teenagers. She was twenty-six years old now and the mother of two. For every job, she was competing against fresh-faced young girls who were *actually* teenagers. And while friends like Grace had built second careers as actresses, Carolyn had no plan B.

CHAPTER 10

Nina

Out on Long Island, my mother was so isolated, away from Manhattan and the friends she had made there. I was barely ever at school, so I can't remember her socializing with the other mothers she might have met if I'd attended regularly. The only friend of hers I can recall was Marlene Colgate.

Marlene lived in Manhattan but spent July and August at her family's beach house, just a few miles away from our home. She had four children, all of them my age or younger. Marlene was petite with long reddish-brown hair and freckles, a natural beauty, never overly concerned about appearances. She was a liberal and a free spirit who wore flowing Indian dresses. She'd grown up in New York City, gone to Smith College, and studied ballet. Marlene talked about politics, about making the world a better place, and how we all had to do our part to save the environment. My mother must have been drawn to Marlene because she was so different from your typical buttoned-up Lloyd Neck resident, but I think my mother also enjoyed time with Marlene because they were so different from each other. Even on the beach, my mother was quiet and self-conscious in her modest one-piece. Marlene, by contrast, was re-laxed and confident, wearing her long bohemian dresses and openly breastfeeding her baby on the beach.

Those days with the Colgates were such a breath of fresh air for my mother—and for me, too. When we went to visit them, instead of being just two of us, my mother and I were part of a group. My mother would sit with Marlene, the two of them huddled together on their beach towels, heads almost touching, speaking in hushed voices. Marlene nodded and knitted her brow, putting a hand on my mother's arm, listening to her, reassuring her. Marlene also took my mother's concerns for my health seriously. She offered to introduce us to her own doctor, Dr. James J. Farley, a homeopathic doctor she described as "a genius" and a "real country doctor."

Marlene's eldest boy, Gibby, was the same age as me. Even though we were already old enough to figure out that boys and girls weren't supposed to play together, we made an exception for each other, wading off into the water at the edge of the beach to look for min-nows. Then came Wim, the second boy, two years younger than Gibby and me; Haven, the toddler; and Ted, the baby. For once, I was with a family where I was one of the eldest and where the other children were all close in age. One time, Gibby and I went too far down the beach, and the Colgates' neighbor, an older woman, came out waving a shotgun, telling us we were trespassing on private property. My father came to our rescue; it's the only time I can remember him being with us out at Marlene's.

Malcolm didn't enjoy the beach. He sunburned easily, and pre-ferred being with his friends to spending time with his family. On this one occasion, he stayed for only a short time before he got up to leave, saying something to my mother as he turned to go. I didn't catch the words, but I saw the look on my mother's face: it was one of furious mistrust. I looked over at Marlene. She was also looking at my mother, observing the whole scene, her face furrowed with concern. As I remember it, Marlene's reaction was one of the only times someone from outside the family gave me any context for what was happening between my parents. Her worried expression let me know that the way my father behaved was not right; that what was taking place within my family was far from normal.

In November of 1967, at my third-grade parent-teacher conference, I had already been absent so much of the year that it was impossible for my teachers to report accurately on my progress.

"Mrs. Reybold was extremely depressed and described the lengthy medical examinations that have not yet resulted in a diagnosis of Nina's ailments," my teacher wrote. "As far as we can ascertain Nina is keeping up, but it is impossible to know. Mrs. Reybold took additional homework for Nina 'if she is able to do it' but did not take the report card. 'Throw it away,' she said, 'It's useless.'"

In January, the school requested another physical report, so in March I went to see a Dr. Estes at the Sound Shore Medical Group. His recommendation was "full activity." At this point, Dr. Estes sent the following note to our school nurse: "I think I have convinced Mrs. Reybold to return Nina to school. Please advise the school nurse not to call Mrs. Reybold when Nina comes to see her, but give TLC for 5 to 10 minutes and return her to her class. She may only be sent home if she has a fever of 101."

However, by the end of the school year, I had been in school for only ten days in total, so they decided to hold me back and make me repeat third grade. My second time in third grade, I did a little better, but I was still present for only fifty-five days.

In January of third grade, I had another examination with Dr. Estes who found nothing wrong with me and again recommended full activity. That same month, the school nurse, Mrs. McNulty, noted that she had spoken to my mother, who explained that I was just not well enough to attend school because of "an occasional low-grade fever."

By February, the notes report that I was in the care of "another Dr." who was "trying to prove my anemia." That month, we went to visit Dr. Farley, the doctor recommended by Marlene. He gave my mother a handwritten note informing the school that I was now under his care. In his note, Dr. Farley stipulated that I have home teaching as I currently wasn't fit to attend school. A few days later, I had my first session with my teacher, Mrs. Johnston, at my home. The sessions didn't last long. By March 4, my mother was canceling them, claiming I wasn't strong enough.

I remember Dr. Farley very well. His offices were on 178th Street near the George Washington Bridge, at the top of a long, narrow staircase. In the waiting room, the chairs and couches were tattered, with splitting seams, as if all the patients sitting here waiting over all the years had worn them all to pieces. Dr. Farley was from Ireland and had an accent that I couldn't always understand, but even so, I felt safe with him. His belly was large and round, he wore wire glasses on his nose, and his balding head was rimmed with white hair. He was always kindly and smiling when we saw him. My mother felt comfortable with him, too. She said he reminded her of her doctor in Ohio. While the other doctors we visited looked at us skeptically, Dr. Farley was different. He didn't judge us. He believed my mother when she told him something was wrong with me. He listened to us. When we left his offices, my mother always seemed so relieved.

Lying on Dr. Farley's dark green examining table, I could see across the room to his desk area. On the far wall, behind the desk, there was a Norman Rockwell painting of a doctor and a little girl wearing a red hat. The doctor had a stethoscope, and the little girl was holding up a doll so that the doctor could listen to the doll's heart. The girl looked shy, maybe even a little worried. The doctor was an older man, red-cheeked and kindly, with white hair. As he pressed his stethoscope to the doll's chest, he stared up into one corner of the room, just like Dr. Farley as he examines me. I liked the painting very much.

When my school requested another examination by a Board of Education medical officer, Dr. Farley wrote again, this time asking them to kindly hold up the procedure until I had seen another doctor.

"We will have to assume that Nina is being 'illegally detained' unless we receive the proper documentation," the school principal, Mr. Bedford, wrote in April 1969. The school needed official authorization for the home teaching. That same month, Mrs. Johnston wrote in my progress report that since I had missed every single day of the marking period, it was impossible to give a progress report at all. In fact, I had been absent for 138 days and present for only 55 days. "I am forced to consider that Nina does not have the skills necessary to progress to Fourth Grade," Mrs. Johnston explained.

At this point, the school insisted I see a physician approved by the Board of Education. Reluctantly, my mother drove me into Manhattan to visit Dr. Edmund Joyner, the chairman of the Pediatrics Department at Roosevelt Hospital. Dr. Joyner gave me a full physical exam. After that, he sent a note to the school explaining that I was in good health and "capable of taking part in school activities suitable for her age."

My mother conceded defeat and sent me back to school. However, my return didn't last long. One day, I was walking to my desk after collecting an assignment from Mrs. Johnston when my knees buckled under me and I fell. I was sent to the school nurse. As instructed, the nurse did not send me home but returned me to class. Later that day, when I told my mother what had happened, she immediately booked an appointment with an orthopedist. The doctor looked at my X-rays and told my mother it was *possible* my legs had stopped growing. Starting the next day, my mother kept me home again.

On April 24, Dr. Farley sent a letter to my school principal to explain that I was seeing a Dr. Michael Lepore at St. Vincent's Hospital and that the school should arrange for home studies until I was ready to return. My principal had finally reached his breaking point. That May, my mother was summoned to appear in family court charged with unlawfully keeping Robin and me home without cause. Dr. Farley sent a note to the Family Intake Unit of Suffolk County to say that my mother would be unable to attend because "she must take the child Nina, age 9, for treatment of a serious illness to Dr. C. Flood."

A day later, Dr. Farley followed up with a letter to the Suffolk County Department of Correction to explain that "Nina will be out of school for an indefinite period of time."

For now, at least, Dr. Farley and my mother had won the tug-of-war with my school.

Although it's not in the school records, I am almost certain it was Dr. Farley who suggested I have colonic irrigation. Throughout my childhood, my mother was convinced I was constipated—not a day went by without her asking me repeatedly if I'd gone. If I said no, she'd give me a glass of orange juice, and then I would sit on the toilet in the powder room by the kitchen and wait. When my mother heard about colonic irrigation, she was convinced it was the cure I needed. I remember going into the city for the irrigation procedure two or three times. The nurses would make me lie down on a gurney, the cold hard metal beneath my back. I remember the container holding the oil at my side, with the terrifying long tube snaking out of one end and bubbles in the oil that rose to the surface, as if trying to escape. The nurse had to pin me down so that the awful hose could be inserted; she had no sympathy for the terrified little girl who screamed and writhed under her weight as she forced it inside of me. The oil pushing into me caused me terrible pain—thirty minutes of heart-racing agony. My only comfort was a hot water bottle on my stomach. If you read the medical literature on colonic irrigation, you'll learn that no one reputable recommends the treatment for very young children. Not then, not now.

In the school records for that year, there's an article from the *Medical Tribune and Medical News* that someone from the school had clipped and placed in my file. OVER-CONCERNED MOTHER HELD URGENT PEDIATRICS PROBLEM, read the headline. The article described a mother who "projects her own illness onto her child and takes him from physician to physician seeking one who will confirm her diagnosis." This mother "falsely sees her child as ill or exaggerates his sickness." Such mothers should be considered "psychiatric emergencies," the article explained.

THAT SEPTEMBER, I somehow progressed to fourth grade, and the school year of 1969–70 started well enough. But by the new year, I had stopped going to school again, and my teacher, Mrs. Jensen, started coming to the house to tutor me. I took my lessons in the den, wearing my pajamas and lying down on the couch, so I wouldn't overexert myself.

Mrs. Jensen had brown curly hair and a dark blue suit. She was a stern, older lady, but I didn't mind. I looked forward to my sessions with her very much. My days were so long and uneventful, and I was eager to learn. Mrs. Jensen gave me a book on Greek mythology, and I became fascinated by the stories of the gods and goddesses.

One day, when the lesson was over, Mrs. Jensen asked me a question.

"Nina, don't you want to come back to school?" she asked me quietly. "You seem fine to me. I don't think there's anything wrong with you."

"I can't," I told Mrs. Jensen, shaking my head. "I'm not well."

"Why won't you come back?" my teacher insisted. "You can tell your mother you *want* to come back to school."

I started to cry. I wasn't used to being questioned. I didn't want to go back. I needed to stay home with my mother.

"I can't," I repeated through my tears.

My mother must have heard me crying, because she came into the room, her face furrowed with concern. Mrs. Jensen stood up and turned around to face my mother.

"Nina needs to be in school," my teacher insisted. "There is *nothing* wrong with her."

My mother protested. She told Mrs. Jensen about my doctor visits, about my health problems, about how hard it had been for me to keep up with my studies.

Mrs. Jensen repeated that I seemed fine and that I needed to be in school; she raised her voice, her finger jabbing the air.

My mother started to cry. I couldn't bear to see her so upset.

"Don't say that to my mommy!" I told Mrs. Jensen.

I ran to my mother, putting my body against hers.

"Leave my mommy alone!" I shouted at my teacher.

This was not like me. I was such a quiet child; I hardly ever raised my voice. But I was going to defend my mother no matter what.

Mrs. Jensen was taken aback. She looked at me and looked at my mother, and threw her hands up, as if she didn't know what else to say.

"You'll be hearing from the school," my teacher informed us. Then she strode out of the house, slamming the door behind her.

We didn't see Mrs. Jensen at the house again.

I was ten years old. I didn't question my mother's role in keeping me at home. I just wanted to protect her from my teacher, who seemed intent on upsetting us. It was only years later that I realized why Mrs. Jensen had shouted at my mother the way that she did. She was trying to save me.

NOT LONG AFTER the incident with Mrs. Jensen, my mother came into my room in the middle of the night to wake me.

"Nina, get up," she whispered. "We're leaving."

Even in the darkness, I could see the pale oval of her face and her sweet, sad eyes darting with nerves.

I did as I was told.

My mother helped me to pack my sister Jill's little olive-green floral suitcase. With me still in my pajamas, we crept out the door, leaving my father sleeping in his bed. My half sister, Patricia, had left her red-and-white convertible Mustang in our garage for the winter. My mother had the key. We slid into the seats of the Mustang. I held my breath as my mother turned the ignition, and pulled away, the sound of the car tires on the gravel drive so loud I was convinced we would wake Malcolm. But as I looked behind me, the house stayed safely dark.

My mother explained that we were going to Steubenville. To Ohio.

We drove through the night, my mother chain-smoking cigarettes with the window cracked, checking the rearview mirror obsessively; the headlamps of every passing car like searchlights tracking our escape. At some point, we pulled over so we could get gas and my mother could make a phone call. I remember wondering who she was calling. My father, to tell him we'd left? Or was she calling her mother in Ohio to tell her we were on our way? When my mother returned to the car, she didn't explain.

She started the engine and we pulled away again, into the night. I knew I had met my Steubenville relatives—my grandmother, my mother's stepfather, and my aunt and uncle—only once, when I was a baby. I had no memory of them. My mother talked to her own mother and her half sister Joyce Lee on the phone sometimes, but I had no image of them in my mind.

The next time we stopped it was outside a small country motel where we got a room and lay down together, sleeping until daylight woke us. In the sunlit morning, my mother seemed more at ease, and so I began to relax, too. We had breakfast at the motel restaurant. Then we got back in the car. The landscape shifted with our mood, until we were driving through lush green hillsides dappled with light and trees. My mother explained that this was Pennsylvania Dutch country. She pointed out the traditional "hex signs" on the sides of the barn buildings, colorful patterned discs with stars and concentric shapes inside them. The next time we stopped, it was to visit a big red barn store where my mother bought me a book about the hex signs. I remember being fascinated by the symbols, their histories and meanings. With my new book, it no longer felt like we were on the run; we were tourists, a mother and daughter together on an adventure.

Back in the car, my mother explained that it was only a few hours now until Steubenville. I remember wide-open highways with many lanes, tollbooths, driving through tunnels that cut through hillsides. Before long, we were crossing the Ohio River on a wide, low bridge, and ahead of us was Steubenville, the chimney stacks of the steel mills sending rain-colored smoke into the sky. On the other side of the bridge, we drove only a few more minutes before turning the corner onto Pennsylvania Avenue.

The house at number 1416 was painted yellow and white with steps cutting through a grassy slope leading to a small front porch. My grandmother Dorothy came to the door to greet us. She was round and smiling, with hair that was brown streaked with silver, eyes that crinkled, and glasses on her nose, like a grandmother in a fairy tale. She hugged my mother, and then I let her do the same to me, folding me into the soft warmth of her skirts. Grandma ushered us inside.

My mother and grandmother headed straight for the kitchen to begin preparing dinner, chatting happily. In the kitchen above the refrigerator was a picture of a young woman wearing a fur stole, with dark hair and cherry-red lips and a little black hat on her head. My mother explained this was a photograph of my grandmother when she was younger. I thought she looked like a movie star! It was clear where my mother got her good looks. Later on, I ventured upstairs, where I found a small room with a window overlooking the street. Like the other rooms in Grandma's home, it was small and dark and decorated with heavy wooden furniture. Right away, I felt certain this must have been my mother's bedroom when she was a girl. There was a little vanity with a mirror and a wooden chair, so I sat down and examined my reflection. When she was my age, would my mother have looked in this same mirror? I was fair and freckled like my father with light brown hair. I didn't look at all like my mother and my grandmother, with their dark good looks; the only thing I had inherited from them was my high forehead. It felt special, important, that I could be here with her.

I went back downstairs, lured by the smell of brownies baking. I had always sensed that my mother didn't like Steubenville—why else had we never visited?—and yet it didn't seem so bad here.

Then Joe, my grandmother's husband, came home. I knew this was my mother's stepfather. He was a tall, stooped man, with a bald head and eyebrows that went up at angles, meeting in a V at the top of his nose. There were no hugs from my step-grandfather. Instead, Joe nodded his greetings to my mother and went straight to the dining table. My mother followed him silently, and I did the same. Joe sat down at the head of the table. He pulled out his napkin and thrust it under the collar of his shirt with a flourish. Then he picked up his knife in one hand and his fork in the other and held them in his fists, ends propped on the table, waiting to be served. Dorothy came in, dutifully putting a plate of food in front of him. Then Joe took his fork and began to eat, stabbing his food and thrusting it into his mouth. For the rest of the meal, no one said a word. My father never took his meals with us—he always carried his plate into the den so that he could eat on his own—but even so, Joe's silence was shocking to me.

I don't remember my step-grandfather showing any interest in me for the duration of the trip. Whenever he came into the house, it was as if the air shifted and soured, putting everyone on edge, my mother in particular. With Joe in the house, my grandmother's personality changed, too. Usually so cheerful, she quietly submitted to his every demand. Perhaps in the long years of marriage she had learned that protesting wasn't worth the trouble.

I don't remember how long we stayed in Steubenville, maybe two weeks, three at the most. But then, as suddenly as we had left Long Island, we were packing our bags and getting in the car to leave. My grandmother stood on the porch as we pulled away, waving and holding back her tears. Then we drove past the long rows of houses. I was sad to leave Steubenville. Despite Joe's presence, I had enjoyed my time at my grandmother's house. In Steubenville, there were no phone calls from the school, no visits from my teacher. I wonder now why we had to leave. Perhaps my father persuaded my mother to come back. Maybe she couldn't stand to be around her step-father anymore.

Or maybe she had no choice.

Many years later, looking through the school records, I learned that in March 1970, right before our departure for Steubenville, the school nurse, Mrs. McNulty, had reported seeing my mother and me at the local A&P supermarket. Earlier that same day, my mother had called the school to say I was too sick for tutoring. If this was the case, why was I out at the supermarket? Mrs. McNulty wanted to know. Soon after, the principal filed a petition for neglect against my mother on behalf of the school.

"The mother of said child, although financially able to do so, has failed and neglected to provide said child with education," the petition states.

Although my father is named in the petition, my mother is the person "legally responsible" for my well-being, as if my father couldn't be expected to have any responsibility in the matter what-soever.

My mother most likely had to leave Steubenville because she was due to appear in court.

Soon after filing the petition against my mother, the school mysteriously dropped the case. Nothing in the school records con-firms what happened next. Years later, I contacted the Family Court of Suffolk County to see if they had any documents pertaining to my case. They referred me to Child Protective Services, who ex-plained that the petition was never submitted to the court, and therefore they didn't have any records on file.

My guess is that Dr. Farley finally convinced the school that I was legitimately sick, because it was around this same time that I was diagnosed with rheumatic fever.

In many ways, rheumatic fever was the perfect illness to ex-plain away my ailments. Symptoms of the disease can be slight or even nonexistent, but left untreated, rheumatic fever can be dan-gerous and even fatal. In 1970, when I was diagnosed, the pri-mary treatment was bed rest. Dr. Farley explained that I had to build up my strength slowly, as one attack might easily follow another, and the illness can linger, even after the symptoms have disappeared.

My mother now had a legitimate reason for me to stay at home on bed rest and to cancel my home tutoring appointments.

On my school report from June of that year, there is a string of handwritten question marks and then an arrow pointing to the words "absent most of year." The records state that my fifth-grade teacher was Mr. Traverse, but I have no recollection of him whatsoever; I was in attendance for only five days the entire year.

Dr. Farley also prescribed penicillin for the rheumatic fever, which I took on and off for the next two years. I kept taking Congespirin for my repeated colds and infections. When I had sore throats, my mother gave me penicillin for strep. I remember she kept the pill bottles on the glass shelves behind her bathroom mirror, taking them out, then crushing the pills in applesauce for me—I hated to swallow them whole.

It was around this age that I remember going to the bathroom, wiping, and seeing blood on the toilet tissue. I remember screaming for my mother. I was hysterical. I was convinced this was the internal bleeding my mother was always talking about. Or maybe I had cancer. My mother came running, but when I showed her the blood, for once, she was calm and composed. She explained to me that I had just gotten my first period. I was going to have this once a month now. She showed me how to place the pad in my underwear to keep myself clean. I had been so isolated that I had no idea this was something I should expect to happen to me. I remember the relief. This was normal.

MY SISTERS LEFT home as soon as they could. Robin was the first to go. She was only sixteen, but she'd already been running away and asserting her independence from my parents for years. She had pretty much dropped out of school in tenth grade. In the years 1968 to 1969, her school records show she was present in school only seventeen days. Even though she showed up now and then, she had essentially lost interest, and my parents had given up on her. In the spring of 1971, she set out on her own. She briefly worked as a barmaid, a secretary, and a dime store clerk in Westbury at first, not far from our home. Not long after Robin left, Jill moved out, too, heading to junior college in Newport, Rhode Island.

That same spring, Sherman Fairchild passed away. Sherman left my father a considerable amount of money, as well as an education fund for my sisters and me. But life on Long Island would never be the same for my father. He had lost his best friend *and* his social life next door. He fell into a depression and now stayed home most of the time.

With both my sisters gone, I was alone with my parents in the Dream House. I became the small sun around which my mother obsessively revolved.

This was the period when her behavior became more and more difficult to understand, even for an eleven-year-old child. One night, I remember, she came into my bedroom very late. In my room I had posters of cats and kittens, my favorite animals, tacked to the walls.

That night, I woke up to find my mother tearing down the cat posters from the walls.

I begged her to stop. "Why are you doing this?" I pleaded.

My mother was pulling at the pictures with her fingernails.

She told me that she could hear knocking in the walls; that she needed to make sure we were safe.

My treasured posters lay in tatters on the floor.

After she left, I cried myself back to sleep.

CHAPTER 11

Carolyn

Grace's career as an actress had finally taken flight. In January of 1954, she was nominated for an Academy Award for her role in *Mogambo*. Although she didn't win, the nomination ensured that she was now officially famous. That April, she appeared on the cover of *Life* magazine with the headline HOLLYWOOD'S BRIGHTEST AND BUSIEST NEW STAR. She was securing roles in new films almost faster than she could make them. That same spring, she returned to Hollywood to begin shooting *The Country Girl* with Bing Crosby and William Holden. After that, she flew to France to film *To Catch a Thief* with Hitchcock and Cary Grant. When she returned to New York in the fall, in time for the release of *Rear Window,* she was determined to stay for a few months to catch her breath. She had made five films in a period of only eight short months.

There was no doubt that Grace's growing fame created a tension between her and Carolyn. It wasn't that Carolyn was jealous— she was thrilled at her friend's success. It was just that there was a lack of equal footing between them that neither friend knew how to balance. They tried. One night in November of 1954, Grace invited Carolyn and Malcolm to join her at a gala premiere at the Capitol Theatre in New York. This would be a good opportunity not only for Carolyn and Grace to catch up but also for the Reybolds to spend time with Grace's new love interest, the fashion designer Oleg Cassini. Cassini's clientele included the most beautiful women in Hollywood—Marilyn Monroe, Rita Hayworth, and Audrey Hepburn—and that night Grace wore a pale pink satin gown of his design.

Carolyn wore a strapless cocktail dress by Ceil Chapman, a New York designer she loved. Before leaving the Manhattan House, she and Grace had both pulled on short white evening gloves and grabbed small fur stoles to wear around their shoulders now that the weather was cooler. Together, they made the short ride down Broadway to Fiftieth Street. Grace was immaculate in her long gown, her golden hair swept into a chignon. In the past, it was Carolyn who had always known just what to wear, but with her career waning, her confidence was leaving her. She was wearing a shorter dress than Grace's, and the only evening shoes she could find to match her dress were strappy sandals, which she knew weren't exactly the right choice for the colder weather. Should she have worn a full-length gown? Different shoes?

As they approached the theater that evening, a group of photographers spotted Grace and gathered around to capture a picture. It was only natural for Carolyn, as a model, to reflexively smile when she saw a camera lens pointing in her direction, so she stopped to pose.

The following night, when Grace came up to the Reybolds' apartment for dinner, as she often did when she was home in New York,

she brought with her the photographs of the event that had appeared in the newspapers that day, including a picture of Carolyn and Grace as they turned to the photographers, with Malcolm and Cassini to one side. As Carolyn leaned over to look at the photos, she was certain she heard Grace mutter under her breath, "They take all the bows without making the pictures . . ."

Carolyn was so rattled by the comment that she couldn't bring herself to ask Grace to repeat it or explain what she'd meant. She felt Grace was sending her a message: that Carolyn should stop encroaching on Grace's hard-earned spotlight. No other words were exchanged on the subject, but Carolyn couldn't shake the feeling that she had failed her friend. She resolved to walk at least ten paces behind Grace whenever they were out together in the future.

THE EVENING OF March 30, 1955, Carolyn sat at home in her apartment at the Manhattan House, watching the Twenty-Seventh Academy Awards ceremony on television. It was only the third time that the awards had been televised—and for viewers like Carolyn, it was still hard to believe that the events on-screen were actually happening in real time somewhere on the other side of the country. Carolyn watched, riveted, as Grace sailed across the stage of the RKO Pantages Theatre, wearing long white opera gloves to her elbows with a little evening purse swinging in the crook of her arm. In the television's black-and-white blur, Grace's long satin gown looked silvery white, but Carolyn knew it was actually the palest blue. At the last minute before leaving for Hollywood, Grace had knocked on Carolyn's door, asking to borrow a slip to wear under the dress. Carolyn had loaned her a silk one, in yellow, Grace's favorite color, to bring her luck.

After presenting the awards for Best Documentary Short and Best Documentary Feature, Grace returned to her seat in the theater and waited. Best Actress was among the final categories to be announced. Eventually William Holden—who had starred with Grace in *The Country Girl*—came out onstage to present the award. Audrey Hepburn, Dorothy Dandridge, Jane Wyman, and Judy Garland had all been nominated in the Best Actress category alongside Grace, with Garland as the favorite to win. But when Holden opened the envelope, it was Grace's name he read from the card. Carolyn watched as Grace floated up the stairs of the RKO Theatre to claim her prize.

Grace took the statue in her hands and spoke softly into the microphone.

"The thrill of this moment," she said, holding back tears, "keeps me from saying exactly what I really feel. I can only say thank you from the bottom of my heart to all who made this possible for me."

Carolyn remembered the girl she had met all those years ago in New York, in glasses and cardigans, who was so determined to be an actress. Grace had done it. She had achieved her dream. Carolyn was so proud of her friend.

Later that month, when Grace returned to New York from her triumph in Hollywood, she no longer pulled up in her cab at East Sixty-sixth Street and the Manhattan House. Two months earlier, she had moved out of the building and into the new apartment she'd purchased for herself, in a grand old building on Fifth Avenue at Eightieth Street. Grace was a wealthy movie star now, and she needed a home that was more in keeping with the woman she had become. Unlike the Manhattan House, with its low ceilings and modest-sized rooms, the apartment on Fifth Avenue was vast and ostentatious, spanning the entire seventh floor of the building. The ceilings soared; the living room boasted wide views across the park and the Metropolitan Museum of Art. Grace was now mistress of a domain that included four bedrooms, a dining room, a living room, and a library. Although her mother had chosen the drab furnishings at her Manhattan House apartment, Grace declined Mrs. Kelly's help this time. Instead, she hired the society decorator George Stacey, and with Stacey's help, she outfitted her new home with soft silk rugs and French antique furniture in shades of sky blue, ivory, and gold.

For the first time since Carolyn and Grace moved to New York in 1947, they were no longer neighbors. Grace had only moved a mile away, but to Carolyn, the new apartment on Fifth Avenue seemed a universe away from their familiar corner of the Upper East Side in the Sixties. Since leaving the Barbizon, Carolyn had always followed in Grace's footsteps, to Manhattan House, to premieres and parties, but now she recognized that her friend had crossed an invisible barrier beyond which Carolyn couldn't trespass. Grace was famous, but Carolyn would never be. Carolyn's face might appear in magazines, but no one knew her name. She didn't have any lines or awards. She was a mute, a mannequin, a coat hanger, only a little more animated than the life-sized dolls that stood in the windows of the department stores.

She knew her place.

That January, Carolyn appeared in a Viceroy cigarette ad, and for the rest of 1955, her modeling jobs arrived steadily. It was no longer the rush of work she'd experienced during her early years, but she was back in the pages of *Seventeen, Glamour, Mademoiselle, Charm,* and *Modern Bride.* Malcolm was also faring better. He had recovered from his illness, and he had been offered a new job as associate director of marketing at the McCann Erickson advertising agency. The new job made Malcolm happy—and although Carolyn was relieved that the burden of supporting the family no longer fell exclusively to her, it was hard not to miss him when, in the evenings, she found herself alone at the Manhattan House, the children sleeping quietly in their rooms, waiting for her husband to come home from long evenings entertaining his clients.

Twenty blocks north, Grace also found herself waiting—but for whom, she didn't yet know. At the age of twenty-five, she was still single. The relationship with Oleg Cassini had stalled after her parents had intervened (Cassini, like Don Richardson before him, was a divorcé, and therefore considered unsuitable by Mr. and Mrs. Kelly). While Grace had been away making movies, it seemed, every one of her closest friends had gotten married and was having children. A woman of her times, she knew that she was in danger of being left on the shelf. Even the triumph of her Oscar win had been tempered by the knowledge that her time was running out. The night of the Academy Awards, Grace arrived back at her suite at the Bel-Air Hotel and lay down on her bed, her golden statuette beside her.

"There we were," she later recalled, "just the two of us. It was terrible. It was the loneliest moment of my life."

IT WAS A few days after Christmas 1955, the same year as Grace's Oscar win, when the telephone rang at Carolyn's Manhattan House apartment.

"I have something to tell you," Grace said. "Meet me tomorrow."

Carolyn could tell right away that something had happened. Grace sounded jubilant and Carolyn immediately assumed that she had met someone. But nothing could have prepared Carolyn for what Grace told her the next day over lunch at her apartment on Fifth Avenue.

"I'm marrying Prince Rainier!" Grace blurted.

Carolyn had had no idea that her friend even had a new love interest; Grace had kept the entire romance a secret, even from her closest friends.

Now Grace told Carolyn the full story. She had met the prince earlier in the year, while she was in Europe at the Cannes festival. *Paris Match* magazine had arranged a photo shoot with Rainier at his palace in Monaco, just along the coast. That day, the prince gave Grace a tour of the palace gardens. The two exchanged pleasantries, photographs were taken, and then Grace returned to Cannes and the prince to his duties. But the visit had marked the beginning of a secret correspondence between them that would last for the rest of the year. Grace returned to New York and went on with her life, preparing for her upcoming roles and publicizing those films she had already made. Each day, however, she checked the mailbox at her apartment on Fifth Avenue, to see if one of the prince's letters might be waiting, unmistakably stamped with the official red-and-gold seal of the House of Monaco.

As they wrote, Grace and her prince revealed more and more about each other, until it became clear they were in love. Although they had met in person on only a single occasion, Grace took Rainier to meet her parents in Philadelphia for Christmas. Here Rainier asked Jack Kelly for his daughter's hand in marriage. Jack gave his consent. At last, Grace had found a man her parents couldn't reject.

If the engagement seemed at all hurried or impulsive, Carolyn felt she wasn't one to judge. She had met and married Malcolm within six months of their first date; she understood Grace's need to feel swept off her feet. That New Year's Eve, Carolyn celebrated with Grace and the prince, along with Grace's closest friends, at the Stork Club in New York, where Grace and Rainier danced, and everyone raised glasses and made champagne toasts to their future.

The official engagement announcement appeared in the newspapers on January 5, 1956, and a lavish engagement party was held at the Waldorf Astoria later in the month. From the moment of the announcement, the American press wouldn't leave Grace alone. She could no longer walk out of her apartment building without being mobbed by the crowds of photographers and reporters waiting outside. Every newspaper and magazine in the country ran daily updates about Grace, Hollywood's princess, and her wedding plans. Cary Grant had given her a little black poodle, Oliver, as an engagement gift, but as she couldn't walk the dog for fear of being hounded by reporters, Grace loaned him to Carolyn's daughters, Jill and Robin—now four and two. Each morning, the girls went out, in their matching navy-blue coats with silver buttons, to walk Oliver in Central Park with their nanny.

Before the end of January, Grace called Carolyn again, this time from Los Angeles, where she was shooting *High Society,* her final film before the wedding. She had more news. She wanted Carolyn to serve as one of her bridesmaids. Carolyn hadn't wanted to assume that Grace would even be able to invite her to the wedding, let alone include her in the party, but on February 20, when the official announcement of the bridesmaids' names was released to the press, Carolyn's name was among them. Grace's sister and four other friends, including Sally Parrish—now married and called Richardson—would make up the rest of the wedding party.

From the moment of the bridesmaids' announcement in February until early April, when it was time to leave for Monaco, Carolyn was so busy preparing for Grace's wedding that she barely had time for a single modeling job. There were multiple dress fittings for the bridesmaids' gowns, and hats and gloves to collect, wedding and shower gifts to buy, and press interviews and photo shoots to attend.

Then there was the bridal shower to arrange, a task that fell to Carolyn and Sally Richardson. The date for the shower was set for

the last weekend in March, just a few days before Grace's departure for Monaco. The Saturday of the party, Grace arrived at Sally's apartment on the Upper East Side swathed in a giant mink coat, wearing a pink pillbox hat decorated with drooping pink silk roses. Photographers were waiting, and Grace duly turned to the cameras, waved, and smiled before entering the building. The fifteen guests that afternoon included Grace's mother, her sisters, and her sister-in-law, as well as her bridesmaids and Alfred Hitchcock's wife, Alma Reville. Carolyn and Sally served champagne and slices of a cake decorated with tiny umbrellas. Later, Grace opened her gifts, which were piled below a large parasol that Sally and Carolyn had pinned with fresh flowers. Inside the boxes—with their elaborate wrappings and ribbons—were fine French lingerie sets, a pair of the softest white kid gloves, a large beach hat for afternoons on the French Riviera, white leather address books, a fancy belt, and a jeweled box for keeping tissues inside. Hitchcock himself had jokingly sent Grace the gift of a floral shower cap. "Something for your shower," he wrote on the gift tag.

Later that week, Carolyn visited Grace at the apartment on Fifth Avenue, where she was preparing to leave for Monaco. Strewn all around were clothes, shoes, purses, hats and gloves, books and letters, her Oscar statuette, seven years' worth of accumulated possessions. Carolyn did her best to persuade Grace that now that she was going to be a princess, she probably wouldn't need her sensible schoolmarm shoes and tweed skirts from her Barbizon days. But Grace was sentimental about clothing. Even if she was going to start a new life in Monaco, she wanted to keep something of the girl she'd been, a reminder of the past, to take with her into her glowing future.

It was all happening at whirlwind speed. The following week, barely three months after her engagement, Grace left on the ship the SS *Constitution,* bound for Monaco and her prince. Carolyn would join her in Monte Carlo via airplane a week later, Malcolm at her side, the bridesmaid's dress wrapped in layers of tissue paper in her luggage. More than anything Carolyn had wanted to go with Grace on the ship, but Malcolm had put his foot down. Between his job, their two children, and the cost, they couldn't afford to be gone that long. Instead, he arranged for Carolyn to be interviewed about the wedding after she returned from Monaco on NBC's *Home* TV show. In return NBC would pay for the airplane tickets. Fearfully, Carolyn had asked Grace if she minded. Now more than ever, Grace was nervous about her privacy and anxious about any betrayal on the part of her friends. Begrudgingly, Grace agreed to the interview, as long as Carolyn didn't wear her bridesmaid's dress. But Carolyn was still terrified that Malcolm had put her in a situation where she had displeased her friend.

Sally Richardson and her husband, John, were also flying to France, and so the two couples flew together, with a connecting flight from Amsterdam. They arrived a little less than a week before the wedding. From the airport, they took the coastal road to Monaco, climbing through the steep and narrow streets of the town, stores shuttered in the afternoon sun, every building festooned with red and white banners emblazoned with the initials R and G—for Rainier and Grace. Then the car turned into Casino Square, where crowds of gray-hatted reporters and photographers were waiting.

Carolyn had been to Europe only once, for a photoshoot for *Mademoiselle* in Paris, but even so, she had never seen anything quite as glamorous as Casino Square, its matching white stone buildings banked by palm trees and overlooking the ocean. Uniformed porters held out their arms to keep back the crowds as Carolyn, Malcolm, Sally, and John climbed out of their car and up the stone steps to the hotel's lobby, gleaming with white marble floors and gilded mirrors on every wall. Upstairs in their room, a giant bouquet of peonies, roses, gladioli, and tuberoses was waiting with a card from the prince welcoming them to Monaco. Thick envelopes arrived inscribed with their names, each one with an invitation or set of tickets to wedding events planned for the week.

First on the agenda was the dinner dance hosted by Grace's parents at the next door Casino de Monte Carlo. The following night there was a white-tie gala at the International Sporting Club in Monte Carlo, with a special performance by the ballerina Tamara Toumanova. Monday was the wedding rehearsal at the Cathedral of St. Nicholas, with a dinner at the palace for the bridesmaids and husbands. And the day before the religious wedding at the cathedral, the civil ceremony was to take place at the palace, where Grace would become Rainier's legal wife, followed by a garden party to which the entire population of Monaco had been invited.

ON APRIL 19, 1956, Carolyn woke early in her room at the Hôtel de Paris in Monte Carlo. She walked over to the hotel windows, parting the thick swagged drapes and swinging open the long, tall windows so she could step out onto the hotel balcony. It was only dawn, and a pink light was creeping across the horizon and the Port Hercule, Monaco's small harbor, with its neat rows of white yachts rocking in place. Beyond the harbor she could see Le Rocher—the rocky promontory on which the prince's palace stood—jutting out into the vast dark Mediterranean. Even after a week in Monaco, the view still caused her to catch her breath, the morning light now revealing dusky-colored buildings clustered on the cliffsides surrounding the harbor and narrow roadways stretching up into peaked green hills. No wonder Grace had fallen in love, not only with her prince but with his country. Carolyn felt as if she could stay here forever.

She stepped back into the room where Malcolm lay sleeping. She had work to do, her hair to fix, makeup to apply. In her seven years of modeling, there had been no role more important than that of Grace's bridesmaid. The dress that Grace had picked out for her attendants to wear was hanging in the closet. Rather than the usual frilly outfits worn by bridesmaids, Grace had selected something modern and distinctive, made from the softest silk organdy in a pale yellow shade that the dressmakers dubbed "Sunlight." It had a high pointed collar and five covered buttons down the front, a pleated sash at the waist, and full sleeves that ballooned out to midforearm. The taffeta skirts were so full that they billowed, the fabric at the back creating its own train.

It had taken two fitting sessions at Grace's apartment on Fifth Avenue before the dresses fit to perfection. The six bridesmaids and Grace's maid of honor—her sister Peggy—had been warned not to put on a pound or gain an inch between then and the wedding. But in the short weeks that followed, Carolyn had been so nervous she had actually lost weight. Now, on the morning of the wedding, her main concern was that the bridesmaid's dress was hanging too loosely around her frame. She hoped no one would notice.

Carolyn was dressed and ready by the time the limousines from the palace arrived to collect her. They drove directly to the palace, and the six bridesmaids—along with Grace's maid of honor— gathered in the white-and-gold salon adjacent to Grace's room holding their posies of tiny yellow rosebuds wrapped in lace and trailing yellow ribbons. When Grace finally emerged from her dressing room, she all but glowed in the palace's half-light. She was already in her white gown, its lace bodice fitted with long sleeves covering her arms all the way down to the backs of her hands, the skirts forming a voluminous pouf of taffeta and lace, and behind her, almost a hundred yards of tulle for a train. Her hair was pulled back in a chignon, the style that Carolyn had always thought suited her best, a lace cap with its white veil attached on her head.

Grace embraced every one of her bridesmaids, and then they walked out together onto the Galerie d'Hercule, the long terrace overlooking the palace courtyard, for photographs. Grace's four little flower girls and two ring bearers were also there, and the main photographer was Grace's favorite, Howell Conant, whom Carolyn also knew from modeling assignments. With Howell directing, Grace and her attendants arranged themselves in groups under the arches of the long gallery. As they posed for their pictures, Carolyn found she couldn't take her eyes off her friend, and not only because Grace looked so beautiful. Far from home, Carolyn was still the girl from Steubenville, always worried she might make another error or misstep. All she wanted today was to do the right thing, say the right

thing, not to embarrass Grace in any way. She kept her eyes trained on Grace, looking for cues. Along with the formal photographs, Conant also captured more intimate, candid moments that day, such as the one where Grace, with a friend's solicitous care, turned to Carolyn and adjusted her hat.

Below in the courtyard, a Rolls-Royce was waiting to drive Grace and her father to the cathedral for the religious ceremony. The bridesmaids waved good-bye, walking the short distance across the courtyard, out into the palace square, its tall shuttered buildings painted in shades of pink, under an arched passageway, and down the short slope that led to the cathedral. A breeze was rising up from the Mediterranean, and each bridesmaid kept a hand to her head to stop her hat from flying from her head.

By the time they approached the grand steps of the cathedral entrance, Grace had already arrived with her father, and the large silk canopy erected outside the church looked as if it were about to be swept away. A cordon of honor of soldiers and sailors from British, French, Italian. and American ships waited in their smart lines. Together, the bridesmaids lifted their skirts to carefully climb the red-carpeted steps leading up to the church. Grace would follow.

Inside it was cool and dark, with baskets of white snapdragons hanging from chandeliers. Every pew in the church was full, the altar ahead lit by tall white candles and decorated with white hydrangeas, lilacs, and lilies. The six bridesmaids began to process, walking slowly in time to the solemn music from the cathedral organ, passing row after row of waiting guests and taking their places in the row of seats to the right of the altar.

Looking across at the crowd, Carolyn could see the cathedral was filled with dignitaries and celebrities. The Aga Khan and King

Farouk of Egypt were in the front row, with Aristotle Onassis close behind. Gloria Swanson, Ava Gardner, and David Niven had flown in from Hollywood. Malcolm was a seat away from Cary Grant and his wife.

But the main attraction was, of course, Grace. She entered on her father's arm, each guest turning as she passed. At every corner of the cathedral stood the giant cameras sent by MGM, a constant reminder that this was the first wedding ceremony to be broadcast live to millions via television.

Grace looked solemn and tense under her veil, with the eyes of the world watching.

Prince Rainier, in accordance with royal custom, arrived last.

Then the sermon began. Mass was offered. The church's organs and choir filled the cathedral with sound. There were prayers and a message from an emissary sent from Rome by the pope. Rings were exchanged, Rainier fumbling to put the band on Grace's finger, and Grace helping him to slide it on.

Then, when the ceremony was over, Grace and Rainier walked arm in arm back down the aisle, the bridesmaids following, exiting onto the cathedral steps and into an explosion of sunlight and applause. Here were crowds of people cheering, everyone waving, craning their necks for a better view. Grace and Rainier walked down the steps and climbed into an open-topped Rolls-Royce. The bridesmaids were ushered into limousines, so they could follow Grace and Rainier in their motorcade. Church bells were ringing out across the city. Ahead, Grace and Rainier's car proceeded slowly through narrow streets. In her car, Carolyn waved back to the smiling people on the route; they were hanging from every balcony and window.

Monaco tradition dictated that along the way, Grace would stop at the chapel of Sainte Dévote to lay her bridal bouquet at the martyr's feet. Grace and Rainier arrived before noon at the small chapel nestled into the craggy cliffs overlooking Monaco's harbor. Young girls wearing the traditional Monaco dress of white blouses and red-and-white-striped skirts waited in rows on the chapel's steps.

Dévote was Monaco's patron saint. She was a young Christian girl born in Corsica in the third century who had devoted herself to the service of God. When the Romans began persecuting Christians, Dévote refused to renounce her faith and she was stoned to death. Her body was placed on a funeral pyre, but her supporters saved her from the flames and put her remains on a boat bound for Africa, where they hoped she would receive a Christian burial. During the crossing, a dangerous storm threatened the boat and its sailors. Then a small gray dove flew from Dévote's mouth and guided the boat to Monaco, where the ship finally ran aground. Local fishermen rescued Dévote's remains, and a small chapel was built in the harbor in her honor. Over the centuries, Dévote was credited with many miracles. She had protected Monaco from invaders and the plague, she ended the Spanish occupation, and each year she made flowers bloom in winter in time for her saint's day.

With Rainier at her side, Grace walked up the steps to the statue of the saint outside the chapel, laying her bouquet of lilies of the valley at Dévote's feet. Grace crossed herself, then knelt for a prayer. Carolyn watched as the princess—Grace was royalty now—descended the steps, climbing back into her waiting car with her prince, pulling away toward the palace, her subjects, and her new life.

On the one hand, Carolyn was elated for her friend. On the other, she knew that Grace's wedding was an ending as much as a beginning. In the past, Grace had always come and gone from Carolyn's life. When they lived at the Barbizon, Grace would go away for weeks at a time, back home to Philadelphia or for summers on the New Jersey shore. After she started her career in movies, she was always flying off to film shoots in Hollywood or somewhere else in the world. But until now Grace had *always* come back. Grace adored Manhattan; so did Carolyn. It was part of their bond. But how could New York ever compete with the beauty and charm of Monaco? Or a palace and a prince? Carolyn knew as she waved good-bye to Grace that she was watching her friend start a new journey, unlike any in the past, one from which she couldn't easily return.

CHAPTER 12

Nina

Midway through what would have been my fifth grade year, the school renewed its interest in my case. Why hadn't I recovered from the fever yet? In February of 1971, the school principal, Mr. Bedford, called our home to speak to my mother, and I answered. My mother was out, and I was home by myself. Since the incident at the A&P supermarket—where the school nurse had seen us and the school filed the petition for neglect against my mother— I usually stayed at home whenever she had go to the market.

"How are you today, Nina?" my principal asked.

"Pretty good," I answered, immediately realizing that was the wrong answer. I panicked and corrected myself. "Well, I mean, not so good."

There was a pause on the other end of the line. I knew that it was wrong to lie but that I couldn't tell him the truth either. I can still recall the queasy feeling in the pit of my stomach, the shame that I couldn't yet put into words.

Mr. Bedford told me to give my mother a message: he expected her to return his call as soon as she could.

Of course, my mother didn't call back, so the next day Mr. Bedford telephoned again. This time, my mother answered. She told him about her own stomach problems, that she was going to the hospital on Monday for treatment and that it was possible I had the same issues, inherited from her, that I couldn't return to school just yet and that she didn't feel I was ready to start home tutoring either. She was very concerned.

The summer before sixth grade, my school assigned a teacher to tutor me at home so that I could try to catch up before the beginning of the year, but by then my mother had found a tick bite on my body, and I spent the summer in bed with tick fever.

That September, the first day of school loomed ahead of me. I always dreaded the first day back. I can still remember the feeling of rising panic in the pit of my stomach as I thought about the school bus pulling in to the circle in front of our school. I didn't have friends at school; I wasn't part of any friendship group because I was never there. The other kids teased me, calling me names.

I remember standing in our laundry room the day before my first day of sixth grade. My mother was quietly folding the clean clothing; the air in the laundry room was warm, and the washing machine hummed its familiar tune, but I was worried. I had just climbed the stairs and was a little out of breath, so I decided to put my hand on my chest. I could feel my heart pounding wildly beneath my fingers; I'd never felt my heart racing like this before. I tugged at my mother's blouse, getting her attention. I asked her if she could hear my heart beating, and she said yes. Then she put her hand to my chest. I could tell from her expression that something was very wrong.

The next day we drove into Manhattan to see a cardiologist. I don't remember anything about his assessment of me, but I do know that my mother was so worried about my heart problem, I didn't go to school for the rest of the year.

By now, a pattern had been established. My mother kept me home from school, which meant that I was afraid to go to school, which meant I then colluded with her to make sure I didn't have to go to school. We were trapped in this vicious cycle together.

MEANWHILE, IN PHILADELPHIA, Robin was in trouble. That November, on my twelfth birthday, my eighteen-year-old sister was arrested at an anti–Vietnam War protest for "contemptuous display" of the American flag. She had been seen with a group of people who were dragging the Stars and Stripes along the ground. I knew about the antiwar marches and demonstrations because I had seen them on the news; now I learned that my sister had joined the movement. Like so many young people at that time, Robin was passionate about ending a war that had already sent tens of thousands of young American men to their deaths. Later, I learned that my sister was writing volumes of poetry and song lyrics about the injustices of the times. After her arrest, Robin pleaded not guilty but was sentenced to pay a fine of fifty dollars or serve five days in jail. She spent one day and one night in jail, at which point the father of a friend of hers paid the fine. Robin was released, but the experience of being arrested didn't stop her from protesting; quite the opposite. She became a volunteer for Vietnam Veterans Against the War. She had ambitions to be a singer-songwriter, and was playing her guitar and performing at protests up and down the East Coast.

The following year, Robin caught bronchial pneumonia. At the same time, a childhood neck problem had flared up again, and she was scared; her breathing was constricted and it was causing her to black out. She had seen multiple doctors, but no one seemed to be able to help. On April 5, 1972, she called my mother to tell her she wasn't getting any better. My mother told her to come home immediately, but Robin refused. She didn't want to see our father; they weren't speaking to each other. My mother was frantic: the rift between my father and Robin was tearing our family apart and endangering Robin's health.

Right there on the phone, my mother came up with a plan to fix things. We were going to leave Long Island and move to France. Although she had no money of her own, a twelve-year-old daughter in her care, and no means of supporting herself, my mother decided this was the only solution. Jill and Robin would come, too. Grace would help us. My sisters and my mother would work there or get support from my father. And while in France, we could go to the holy shrine at Lourdes, where we could all be cured.

Although Grace and my mother kept in touch via letter and the occasional phone call, it had been more than a decade since my mother had last seen the princess. My mother didn't wait to send a note to the palace or telephone to let Grace know we were coming. My father was away on business, so my mother simply seized the window of opportunity. The following day, on April 6, 1972, we went to the bank, where she withdrew three thousand dollars from our family bank account. Then we drove into Manhattan to have my name added to my mother's passport. Jill stayed behind at the house on Long Island to finish the packing. She would meet us in the city the following day. Robin was going to take the train in from Philadelphia.

In Manhattan, my mother left our family car in a parking lot with a note pinned to the windshield for Malcolm to find there. *We need prayer. We need a miracle. I have taken the girls and gone to Lourdes.*

That night, my mother and I stayed at the Barbizon on the Upper East Side. I remember sitting on the bed and talking with my mother, looking out the window. She didn't tell me this was the place she had stayed when she first came to New York. The following day, we went to buy tickets on an ocean liner bound for France; my mother didn't want to fly because of Robin's health issues. The plan was to meet Jill and Robin down at the docks later in the day, but at the last minute, we learned that Jill wouldn't be joining us. My father had returned from his business trip just as Jill was trying to leave with our suitcases. He was refusing to let her go. This was bad news. Not only could my father potentially come into the city to try to stop us now, but Jill had my suitcase with her on Long Island.

I wasn't going to have any of my clothes for France.

I remember my mother taking me to B. Altman's department store on Thirty-fourth Street, where she said I could pick out a pair of pajamas so I would at least have something to sleep in. I chose a short-sleeved yellow pair, dotted with orange flowers, that buttoned down the front. We didn't have time to purchase anything else. We needed to get to the docks as soon as we could.

Robin met us at the pier. She looked so beautiful, with her wide-set brown eyes and long light brown hair. She was wearing a white pantsuit, very fashionable at the time, which made me feel even worse about my lack of any clothing. I was twelve years old and going to live in France without any of my clothes or books. Robin must have sensed I was worried, because the minute she saw me she wrapped her arms around me.

"What do you think?" She grinned. "Ready for an adventure?

I nodded.

Truthfully, I didn't feel ready. Everywhere I looked, there were people carrying suitcases, and I had nothing. I looked down at my little white peasant blouse and my striped woolen dirndl skirt that I'd been wearing since we left Long Island yesterday. I knew the kids at school were right: I looked like a baby. *How can I meet Aunt Grace,* I thought, *when I don't have a pretty dress to wear?*

We joined the long line of passengers waiting to board the boat. The SS *Michelangelo* had a vast, windowless hull and giant funnels rising from its deck. We had a cabin with four bunks in tourist class, at the bottom of the boat. The walls were mint green, and there were no windows. At night, we had dinner in the dining hall. There were de- canters of wine on every table, and I remember being impressed that even the young people were served wine with dinner. Robin explained it was the European way. I had a small sip of wine but didn't like it. Every night we sat at the same table with the same people. I prayed they wouldn't notice I was still wearing the same outfit: my white blouse and striped skirt. I remember feeling a constant and creeping sense of discomfort. Even at the best of times, it was hard for me to talk to people I didn't know—I didn't have any practice at it. When I wasn't with Robin or on the deck with my mother, I read books from the ship's library, curled up in the bottom bunk in the cabin.

Then one day, when we were getting ready to go for dinner, there was a knock on the door. We were being summoned to the purser's office immediately. My mother had a phone call. The purser was standing outside his office in a hallway lined with glass cabinets hold- ing ship's instruments and official documents. He ushered us in- side. I sat down near his desk, watching as he carefully positioned two speakers on the table. Then he pressed a button. The speakers began to crackle and hiss.

"Carolyn, it's Malcolm." I could hear my father's voice through the interference. He sounded furious. "Carolyn, I need you to turn back. When you get to France, you need to turn around and come home, do you hear me?"

My mother looked horrified. She turned to the purser as if to say, *How could you do this to me?*

Another voice was coming through on the second speaker.

"Carolyn, it's Grace," said the voice. I recognized the soft, almost English-sounding accent from the films. "Carolyn, you need to go home to Malcolm. It isn't right. You have to do as your husband tells you."

My mother didn't reply. She looked as if she wanted to run from the room.

My father's voice returned. "Carolyn, when you get to Cannes, just get on the next boat back, do you hear me?"

I could hear the exasperation in my father's voice. This was yet another thing my mother had done that didn't make sense and made *his* life harder. Grace sounded so calm, repeating whatever my father said. They were both on the same side, against my mother. I felt so sorry for her. At the same time, I had a strong feeling that I shouldn't be listening to this conversation, that this should be between the adults.

The boat rocked beneath us. My mother was crying.

"We need a miracle," she said over and over. I went to her and wrapped my arms around her legs.

IN THE COMING DAYS, our ship passed through the Strait of Gibraltar, the waters now deepening to tones of blue, circled by the rocky shorelines of Spain and Morocco, giving us our first sight of land

since leaving New York. After more than a week on board the ship, we pulled in to the port at Cannes, its bright white buildings topped with their rust-red roofs, the skies as bright as the ocean below. My mother explained that Cannes was about an hour's train ride from Monaco. Grace was traveling on official business, so we might not see her right away. Again, I worried about meeting Aunt Grace in my little blouse and skirt.

My mother had studied French in high school, and she managed to find and negotiate the rent on a small garret studio in a seventh-floor walk-up on a narrow street not far from the Croisette, the main road that ran alongside the water. I remember the view of red rooftops stretching out to the ocean. The apartment was old, with pale-colored walls and floral-print bedspreads. It had no kitchen and no heat. Mornings, we went out to one of the little cafés on the Rue d'Antibes for breakfast. My mother would order drinks and food for us; my favorites were the crepes drizzled with chocolate. After we finished eating, it was my job to count out the money to pay for our check. *L'addition,* my mother called it. I loved separating out the shiny francs and centimes into stacks, then putting the correct change in the waiter's little silver tray.

I remember one morning after breakfast, my mother praised me on my ability to count out the francs and centimes. The memory stands out because she rarely complimented me in this way. I think she was usually too worried about me to notice when I learned something new. It was only years later, when I became a parent myself, that I realized how much children need to be encouraged and coaxed to try new things, and how little of this kind of support I received as a child. The expectation from my mother was that I would never succeed at anything because I wasn't strong enough. I was so fearful of the world as a result, such a quiet, solemn child. But I remember actually skipping across the street to go back to our little garret that day. I was filled with pride and happiness because my mother had told me I'd done a good job.

EACH MORNING, after breakfast, our mother smoothed down her hair and, wearing her nicest blouse and skirt, went off to find work. She barely spoke any French, she didn't have papers, and although she had worked in a department store after high school, her only real work experience was as a model. Perhaps she tried the stores along the Croisette that catered to tourists, thinking that her English might be an advantage there, or maybe she thought she could find work as a waitress. Robin also tried to look for work, but without knowing any French at all, the task couldn't have been easy.

In the afternoons, Robin and I went down to the narrow beach, with its blue-and-white-striped umbrellas, and although I didn't have a bathing suit, I would sit on the warm sand as Robin basked in the sun in her bikini. Then I'd walk down to the water to dip my toes, always trying not to stare at the women sunbathers with their bare breasts. I had never seen anything like it! My sister explained that was just what you did in France. In the evenings, Robin went out dancing at the local nightclubs, and I lay awake, worrying that something had happened to her. She always returned, but often not till dawn.

After only a week in France, money was already running low. My mother called my father, but he refused to send us funds. We had spent almost all our money on the room in the garret, and Grace was still away. My mother decided it was time to go to Lourdes. She bought us second-class train tickets, and early the next morning we boarded our train bound for southwest France. We watched as the sun rose over the ocean, revealing village after village all along the rocky coastline of the Côte d'Azur. Soon we were barreling through tunnels and valleys, the ocean behind us now, a new, greener landscape ahead.

Lourdes had always held a special place in my mother's heart. Her favorite film was *The Song of Bernadette*, about the life of the nineteenth-century saint Bernadette Soubirous. Whenever *The Song of Bernadette* played on television, we watched the movie together, sitting close to each other in our den. The film starred Jennifer Jones, one of my mother's favorite actresses, and it told the story of Bernadette, a young peasant girl living in Lourdes more than a hundred years ago. One day, Bernadette was collecting firewood in the caves near her home when she saw a vision of a beautiful lady dressed all in white and wearing a white rosary. When Bernadette went back to the caves again, the beautiful lady spoke to her. The lady explained that she was the Virgin Mary and she asked Bernadette to build a chapel there on top of the caves. On the next visit, the lady asked Bernadette to dig in the ground and drink from the spring there. Soon a stream was flowing from the cave, and although the water was muddy at first, it soon cleared. Water from the stream was given to the sick, and those people were miraculously cured.

But not everyone believed in Bernadette's visions, and people began saying she was insane. The Church launched an investigation, and Bernadette was called in front of a tribunal. Eventually, the local bishop declared that "the Virgin Mary did appear indeed to Bernadette Soubirous." Bernadette was vindicated, and a large white statue of the Virgin Mary was placed in the caves and a church was built above. Since then, millions of people from around the world, sick or suffering, had come to Lourdes on a pilgrimage, hoping to be cured.

WE ARRIVED AT Lourdes late at night. My mother found us a room in a small pension not far from the river. In the morning, we woke early to the sounds of church bells echoing and a soft mist hanging over the town. Ever since leaving New York, my mother had been tense and distracted, but now she was calm, as close to happiness as I can remember her. We were finally in Lourdes, and the shrine, she believed, would change our lives. After breakfast, we made our way past the cathedral and down to the river. Crowds were gathering, everyone walking in the same direction, people in wheelchairs or walking with canes, the elderly and the sick, holding on to family members and friends. All along the river there were stands selling figures of Mary and bottles of holy water.

My mother had been brought up Methodist, but Catholicism fascinated her. Her birth father had been Catholic, and when she visited him as a teenager, she had attended a Catholic summer camp. From a young age, she had fallen in love with the dramatic stories of the saints, and she had a special affection for the Virgin Mary. Part of her bond with Grace—who was born a Catholic— was that her friend had taken Saint Bernadette as her patron at her confirmation.

We went down toward the river and across a small bridge. On every side of us, people were walking silently. We could hear singing ahead. In the near distance, we could see a church perched on a bluff, with deep crevices in the craggy rock below. I knew immediately that this was the grotto where Bernadette saw her visions of the Virgin Mary. We followed the crowd through the gates toward the hollowed cave. Above us, there was a giant white statue of the Virgin Mary, her hands pressed together in prayer, a trickle of water wetting the stone directly below her feet. The people ahead of us went up to the rock and started running their hands along it. Some had brought bouquets of flowers as offerings to the Virgin. Others sat on rows of seats, as if in a church, or stood lost in their thoughts or prayers.

My mother walked toward the Virgin, her hands clasped. I could see she had tears rolling down her cheeks. Robin and I were right beside her. We had come all this way. It couldn't be for nothing. I waited for the change to sweep through me. I screwed up my eyes, pressed my hands together, and asked Saint Bernadette and the Virgin to take care of me, my mother, and my family. *Please make Robin better. Please make my mother happy. Please just let everything be okay.*

Later in the day, we collected holy water from the little faucets in the rock face, taking sips from our bottles. By the time we left Lourdes the following day, my mother was convinced that we were cured and that a new chapter in our lives was about to begin. But

Robin was still unwell. We saw various doctors in Cannes, including a chiropractor and a general practitioner. We visited the English hospital, where she saw a specialist, but by now, there was no money left to pay for medicine. My mother called the palace in Monaco, hoping that Grace was back from her trip and could help us. Grace's secretary explained that Grace was still away but that the princess wanted to do whatever she could to help. Eventually, an arrangement was made: the secretary would meet my mother and lend her the money for our passage home. My father would repay Grace as soon as he could.

The secretary gave my mother an address, and we went there directly. It was an apartment in Nice, near the waterfront, large and glamorous. There were mirrors on every wall redoubling the sunshine outside, and there seemed to be something made of silver on every surface—silver candelabra, silver picture frames, silver statuettes. Outside the windows the waters of the Côte d'Azur glinted their response. Did the apartment belong to the princess? Or one of her friends? I can't remember. The secretary gave my mother an envelope with the money inside; then we left the apartment and returned to the waterfront. (The following year, my father repaid my mother's debt, while he was on a business trip in Europe.) With the money loaned us by Grace, I could finally buy a new outfit. I remember Robin and I wandered the back streets of Nice looking in the little stores and boutiques for something I liked. Robin helped me pick out mauve-colored brushed-cotton jeans with a matching long-sleeved T-shirt decorated with Indian-style embroidery. I loved that my new outfit looked just like something Robin would wear. I felt older, more sophisticated, no longer the baby.

I never did get to see Aunt Grace while we were in France. The following day, my mother bought us tickets on the SS *Raffaello*, leaving from Cannes and bound for New York. I'll never know for sure what was going through her mind that day as she stood on the ship's deck, watching the red rooftops and sparkling white buildings of Cannes recede from view, but I can imagine. As the boat tugged its way through the waters, leaving France behind in its wake, with every second that passed, she was being carried back to Long Island, to the Dream House, where Malcolm was waiting.

CHAPTER 13

Carolyn

It was always the case that what my father wanted was not what my mother would have chosen. In 1957, the year after Grace's wedding, Malcolm announced he was no longer satisfied with the apartment at the Manhattan House. He wanted more space, more light, more air. The other executives at McCann Erickson lived out in the suburbs with their families. At a certain point in your life, it was what you did as a man of stature and class: you moved out of town. By now, Jill and Robin were six and four; they needed a yard and their own bedrooms. Malcolm's closest friend, Sherman, was offering to gift the family five acres of waterfront property adjacent to his estate on Long Island. The setting was spectacular, shadowed by woods on both sides, with views of the Sound and its own small beach. They could hire an architect to build the Dream House there.

Malcolm was convinced it was a good plan, but Carolyn wasn't so certain. She had visited Sherman's estate over the years and knew it was isolated, thirty minutes' drive from the nearest train station

and across a causeway that made you feel as if you were leaving the rest of the world behind. She was worried she would miss the city. She loved their apartment at the Manhattan House. To her it didn't seem cramped; it felt cozy. After six years of motherhood, she had settled into a happy routine with the children and their nanny, relying on their schedules for the quiet rhythm and predictability of her days. In the city, she had everything she needed. There was Central Park close by, Bloomingdale's, the ballet, her friends, all within a few blocks. Malcolm reassured her that she could go into Manhattan whenever she liked. It was only a train ride away; she could have the best of both worlds! Besides, he had already picked out an architect, Randall Cox, well known in the South and an up-and-comer on the East Coast. Together, the two men had started drawing up the plans.

Cox's vision for the new house was a modern, barn-shaped building constructed from redwood and glass, very much in the contemporary style. The main living area would be expansive, with a lofted ceiling two and a half stories high and glass picture windows opening out onto the views of the Sound. Carolyn worried that with all that space and glass right on the water's edge, the house was going to feel cold, especially in winter. If they were going to move out of the city, she was hoping for something homier, more like a cottage, a place where she could be comfortable with the children, somewhere like Steubenville, where neighbors lived close by and watched out for one another. Carolyn's roots were simple. Malcolm felt that she was missing the point. Sherman's estate was on Long Island's Gold Coast, where millionaires came to spend their summers. Besides Sherman's castle, there was the Colgate estate, the Marshall Field estate, the Wood estate, vast mansions built on acres of manicured land. The Reybolds were going to have to find their own way to keep up with the neighbors. They needed to build a show house, a statement of good taste, a place where you could invite people for parties. For Carolyn, though, the neighbors were part of the problem. Whenever she went to out to visit Sherman on Long Island, she was reminded yet again that she was an outsider, the imposter from Steubenville.

But Malcolm was determined, and it became harder and harder for Carolyn to resist getting swept up in his enthusiasm and plans. She was happy for him that he seemed so excited about the project. Perhaps if they moved to Long Island, it would be a new start, a chance for them to be closer as a couple. Perhaps Long Island would be good for their marriage.

So in the summer of 1958, Carolyn began packing up the apartment at the Manhattan House. As she filled boxes with their belongings, her thoughts turned to Grace, who had helped them find the apartment in the first place. It seemed like yesterday that Grace

had boxed up her own life to leave Manhattan and move to Monaco. Two years later, so much had happened. Grace had given birth
to a daughter, Caroline, and then a son, Albert. Little Caroline had
been named for a relative of Prince Rainier's but with a nod to
Grace's old friend, and Carolyn had been deeply touched by the
gesture. She missed her friend. They had seen each other only twice
since Grace's departure, when Grace came to back to visit New York
en route to see her family in Philadelphia. In between, they wrote
to each other.

Now Carolyn wrote Grace to tell her that they were moving,
out to Long Island, to Rose Cottage, a guesthouse on the Colgate
estate, not far from their plot of land so they could more easily
supervise the building of the Dream House. It wasn't as if Carolyn
needed to come into the city for work anymore. Since Grace's
wedding, she had worked only four modeling jobs, and Eileen
Ford had removed her name from the agency's books. Now that
she had turned thirty, she could no longer pass for a teenager; she
knew that her career was over. As much as she missed modeling,
Carolyn's focus now was getting the family settled out on Long
Island, and helping the girls get adjusted to their new elementary
school when they started in the fall. Malcolm was absorbed in su-
pervising the work on the new house, which he hoped would be
ready within the year. The move to Long Island was going to be a
fresh start.

Then, in the spring of 1959, Carolyn wrote to Grace with good
news. She was pregnant again, due in November. That summer at
Rose Cottage, Carolyn began to feel the first stirrings of the baby
inside her. Work on the Dream House was progressing well, and
before Jill and Robin went back to school in September, the family
finally moved in, unpacking their boxes. The girls spent the final

days of vacation roaming on the beach and in the woods next to the house. Malcolm was thrilled, so proud of his new home. Jill and Robin were excited to have their own rooms.

Carolyn watched as the leaves slipped from the trees, fall shifting into winter. Her due date came and went, the baby getting bigger and heavier with every passing day.

When her water finally broke on November 22, 1959, Malcolm was out, socializing at Sherman's. Snow was falling, covering the trees surrounding the house in a thin mask of white. Carolyn called her husband to tell him she needed to go to the hospital.

At Huntington Hospital, Carolyn was put in a gown, prepped for surgery, and wheeled into an operating room. She had always known that she was going to have another C-section. In those days, if you'd had a prior caesarian, you didn't have the option of delivering any other way.

After the anesthesia was administered and Carolyn was no longer conscious, the doctor took his scalpel and made a long, vertical incision starting from above the belly button, working his way through fat and muscle until the abdomen was fully opened. The surgeon then cut into the womb, so that I could be brought into the world.

I was a large baby, ten pounds ten ounces, fine and healthy. The mother on the operating table was another matter. Right away, the surgeon could see that the uterus was extremely stretched out from carrying such a big baby; it wasn't contracting in the way that it should after a delivery. He tried to massage it to help it to contract, but nothing was working. Carolyn was beginning to hemorrhage. This was an emergency. The surgeon was going to have to remove the uterus in order to save her life, an extremely complicated and risky procedure. The womb was connected to Carolyn's body by a complex network of blood vessels; it wasn't going to be possible to remove all of it. The surgery took more than two hours, with the surgeon having to repeatedly clamp and suture to stem the bleeding.

When Carolyn woke up from the surgery, she was told that she'd had a baby girl, and hysterectomy.

She stayed in the hospital for more than a week after the surgery, doing her best to recover. The first few days, she could barely roll over or sit up without help. Her abdomen was black with bruising, and there were thick staples holding her middle together. She had lost so much blood during the surgery that when she finally looked in the mirror it was as if she were staring at her own ghost. When she coughed, the pain was so excruciating she thought her insides would spill out. She wasn't able to stand up to visit the baby nursery, so the nurses brought me to her bedside. But my mother was so weak, it was hard for her to hold me. Each day, the nurses asked my mother for a name to put on the birth certificate, but Carolyn was too exhausted to decide.

Malcolm barely came to visit. Carolyn knew he was disappointed. He had been hoping for a boy. She'd even put a little blue blanket with a white ribbon trim in her overnight bag, convinced that she would be able to give him what he wanted. Malcolm may have decided on my sisters' names but he showed no interest in choosing mine.

For an entire week, I remained nameless. The nurses felt so bad for me that they spent as much time holding me as they could, and they gave me the nickname Cuddles. Then, the night before my mother left the hospital to go home, she had a dream about a young French girl carrying schoolbooks and wearing a trench coat. My mother decided to give me a French-sounding middle name—Suzanne. My first name would be Nina, meaning "grace."

CHAPTER 14

Nina

Not long after we returned from our France trip in the spring of 1972, Jill brought home a friend, Marcia, from college. It was a weekday, and I remember I was sitting in the den, watching TV, wearing my yellow and orange pajamas I had picked out to take to France.

Marcia came into the room and looked at me coolly. "Why are you not in school?" she asked.

It was a good question, even if I hated the judgment it implied. Why *wasn't* I at school? Anyone could see I was healthy! Even my mother believed I had been cured at Lourdes! I was twelve years old, and under Marcia's cool gaze, I felt ashamed. For the first time, I acknowledged to myself that it was *wrong* for me to be home all the time.

Meanwhile, my mother was directing her attention elsewhere, completely preoccupied with Robin, who still wasn't well. No longer my mother's primary concern, I seized my opportunity for freedom. Jill was working as a mother's helper during her summer vacation for a family out in the Hamptons. I decided I wanted to spend as much of the summer as I could at the beach with her.

Amagansett was about a two-hour drive from our home, but it was as far from my mother as I had ever ventured. Jill was almost twenty and living independently from our parents, working, studying, and with her own social life. To a twelve-year-old, she was impossibly grown-up and independent, with her long, straight brown hair, parted in the middle in curtains, and her stylish clothes. We had a lot of fun that summer. I think Jill knew exactly how restricted my life had been until now, and she felt a responsibility as my elder sister to show me the world. With Jill's encouragement, I got my own babysitting job, taking care of an eighteen-month-old for a couple who lived nearby. The first day I was terrified. My mother had never encouraged me to have any responsibility whatsoever—homework or even the smallest household chore was considered too strenuous— but Jill kept reassuring me that I could do it. And I did; I took care of that baby, and I did a great job. Next, Jill asked me to help with the newspaper route she had, and soon I was waking up at 4:00 A.M. and delivering papers around the neighborhood. I remember Jill telling me that an independent person could stand on one leg and rest the opposite foot on the other knee. I tried it out, nearly toppling over in the process, but laughing as I finally managed to right myself.

This was the year my body started to change. Almost overnight, I went from being flat-chested to having small breasts. I had to beg my mother to buy me a training bra. That summer, I borrowed a bikini from Jill to go down to the beach because the white two-piece my mother had purchased for me earlier in the year was already too revealing. After I got paid for my babysitting work, I remember going to a boutique in East Hampton and buying myself a new bikini in pink, navy, and purple.

The weeks went by in a haze of working, enjoying myself with Jill, and spending time at the beach, until I had been away from my mother for almost a month. On my last day in Amagansett, I remember, we went to the beach for the entire day. The next day, I arrived back at my parents' house with a bright pink sunburn across my shoulders and back. My mother was furious with Jill for not taking better care of me, but for the first time, I felt defiant. When my mother insisted I stay on the couch covered in Solarcaine, I refused. I didn't want her to fuss over me anymore. The sunburn would fade, and I would be fine—and besides, it was worth it to stay at the beach all day with Jill.

THAT SEPTEMBER, I started junior high in a new school. I can still remember the outfit I wore for my first day: a white piqué halter top and white cutoff jean shorts, with a tan suede belt with a gold lion buckle given to me by Jill. For the first time, I was actually excited about starting a new school year. I had missed every single day of sixth grade, but seventh grade was going to be different. Students at this junior high came from all over the district, which meant that most of them wouldn't know me. They had no idea I was the "baby" who had stayed home for most of elementary school because I was sick.

At junior high, I could start again.

While most of the kids on their first day at a new school were looking for familiar faces, I was looking for anyone who *didn't* know me or my history. I remember looking across the room and noticing a girl at the center of a group of other students. Like me, she was tall and slim and had very long, wavy brown hair. We ended up sitting next to each other. Her name was Diana, and we clicked right away. I started spending as much time as possible with my new friend, often going back to her home after school.

Diana's family was so different from mine. Her father was the superintendent at the Cold Spring Harbor High School, and unlike my father, he actually came home each night for dinner. Diana's mother would bake cookies for us; she was the PTA president and was very involved at school. The family went to church on Sundays, and I went with them more than once, envying the feeling of belonging and acceptance that the services seemed to offer. Even little things at Diana's house felt new to me. I remember the smell of Herbal Essence shampoo and conditioner in the bathroom. How could a shampoo smell so good? I spent as much time at Diana's house as I could.

THAT FALL, my mother was still distracted. Robin was in trouble again. My sister had received a call to say that she was under investigation by the welfare department. Robin had been claiming emergency welfare payments since earlier in the year, when she fell sick and had been unable to work and pay her rent. Unfortunately, she had lost her wallet on a visit back to Long Island, and a newspaper reporter had found it. The reporter, seeing that Robin had food stamps and her welfare card alongside her landing card from the trip to France, decided to look into her case. He had called the welfare office asking questions, which triggered an inquiry.

The reporter returned the wallet to my sister, interviewing her and my mother about what had happened. He told my sister that he was writing a report on how tough it is to live on welfare, but when the article came out that October, it was a very different story. SHE LIVES IN A $100,000 HOME—AND ON WELFARE, the headline read. The article stated that Robin had claimed welfare checks even though she came from a "wealthy" family living in an expensive home and that she had used her welfare money to help fund our trip to France. In the coming days, there were more articles in the paper describing Robin as a "poor little rich girl." One reporter referred to her as "one of a growing number of young people from middle-class backgrounds who have left the security of their homes to be part of a less certain culture."

"I'm being crucified because I'm some politician's idea of a welfare rip-off," Robin told a reporter from *The Philadelphia Inquirer*. At the time she was interviewed, she had just been told that she had to move out of her apartment because her landlord had found out about the scandal and evicted her. The reporter described Robin as "fighting back tears, her long brown hair disheveled."

Robin had become a kind of poster child for the dropout generation. Hate mail began arriving at our home. "When I think that any part of the burden of my taxes goes to support things like you," someone wrote, "I get sick with fear for the future of my country."

Robin was now facing possible fraud charges. The truth was that she had lied about her age when she first applied for welfare; she had told the office she was twenty-one when she was actually eighteen so that she would be eligible for help. In her defense, Robin had been sick; she needed the money and didn't see any other way to get by. She wasn't receiving any support from our parents, and her frequent illnesses meant she was missing work. Without any guidance or supervision from the adults in her life, my teenage sister was lost.

My father blamed my mother for what was happening with Robin, and in turn, my mother blamed my father for forcing us to come back from France. Perhaps the only advantage of this period of turmoil at home was that my mother was too busy to worry about me, which meant I was able go to school each day. I got up each morning, got on the bus, and went to classes. After school I went to Diana's house. I had friends and an actual social life. At the end of the year, Diana was voted "most popular" and I was voted "best dressed."

The seventh grade ended up being the only full year of school I completed while in my mother's care.

In February 1974, Robin's welfare case was resolved and she was required to pay the state back the money she had taken. At this point my mother turned her attention back to her youngest child. The school records indicate that Dr. Farley thought I had either pneumonia or the flu followed by possible appendicitis. In April, he signed my application for Special Educational Services, and I started receiving home tutoring again. The notes show I had lessons with Mrs. Ackerman, my English teacher, Mrs. Griffin for math, and Mr. Johnson for science although I can't recall anything about them. What I do remember is Mr. Finnegan—my young, blond, handsome history teacher—tutoring me while sitting on the edge of my bed. My mother seemed to think it was more important for me to *stay* in my bed than it was to protect me from having a young male teacher in my bedroom.

Soon enough, my mother started calling the school to cancel my tutoring sessions, because I was "too sick for the visits."

Once again, I was alone in the house on Long Island with my books and my thoughts. My sisters were away. My parents were miserable in their marriage. I was back to watching my soap operas and the TV news three times a day. That summer, President Nixon resigned after the Watergate scandal. I was thirteen years old, about to turn fourteen. I was still a child, but I wasn't a baby anymore. I knew the old president was a liar and a new president hadn't even been elected. I was starting to understand that things were very wrong, not only with the world, but right here in my home as well. Although I would never have dared to voice opinions in my father's presence, I was starting to question him, his beliefs, and most of all his treatment of my mother.

IN THOSE YEARS when I still lived at the house on Long Island, I used to have a recurring dream. In the dream, I was standing in the five-and-dime store in Huntington, not far from our home. There was a cash register right in front of me. I knew my mother was near, but I couldn't see her. I had the feeling that something was very wrong. I knew I needed to let someone know what was happening, but when I tried to open my mouth to scream, nothing came out. I had no voice—no way of letting anyone know I was in danger. When I woke up from the dream, I was shaking, the cries still trapped in my throat.

In reality, it was my sister Robin who came to my rescue. Soon after I entered ninth grade in September of 1974, Robin came out to visit us at the house on Long Island. That afternoon, she asked me to take a walk down to the beach so we could talk privately. I took her hand, and we crossed the lawn out to where the inlet gave way to a small crescent of soft beige sand. We sat down, hugging our knees, the breeze sweeping strands of our hair across our faces, looking out across the green-gray waters of the Long Island Sound. In summer, boats would crisscross the waters here, but now that it was fall, we were perfectly alone.

Robin asked about how I was getting along in this new school year. I told her I was working hard to catch up on the work I'd missed toward the end of eighth grade when I'd been out sick. I explained to Robin that I was miserable at home; our parents were barely speaking to one another.

My sister listened. And then she turned to me.

"Nina," she said, "you know, you were *never* sick all those years."

The meaning of Robin's words was impossible for me to process in that moment. No one had ever said anything like this to me before! My mother had told me I had internal bleeding. That I had rheumatic fever. She was my *mother*. Why would she say those things to me if they weren't true? But at the same time, I knew in my heart that Robin would never lie to me.

Robin explained that she had talked to Jill and that they both felt I should leave Long Island. Our parents' marriage was over. They had financial troubles; the Dream House was their only asset. The only way our mother and father could afford to separate was by selling the house, and the only thing that was holding them back was me: they were staying together for my sake.

"Nina, if you leave now it will be better for everyone," Robin told me.

I didn't question my sister. I knew I needed to leave. If I hadn't been sick all those years, then my mother had been doing something *very wrong* keeping me home, and if that was true, then I knew I didn't want to be around her anymore.

I had one decision to make: Did I want to live with Robin or with Jill? That day on the beach, Robin and I talked over my options. I could either go to Philadelphia with her or live with Jill in Manhattan. Robin had a live-in boyfriend, Skip, and I felt I didn't want to be in the way. Jill had graduated from college and could use the help with the rent. Manhattan also seemed like the easier transition; I was familiar with the city, and I would be close enough to still see my friends on Long Island. I decided to go with Jill. In the space of minutes, the decision had been made. I was going to leave home, and this would force our parents to finally separate, something they should have done years ago.

Together, my sisters and I took charge of our family's future.

The next morning at school, in math class, I told Diana the news that I was leaving and moving to New York City. We made a pact that she would come to see me in the city, or I would come out to visit her on Long Island. Our friendship would continue, but with the whole of Manhattan at our disposal.

Although I remember my excitement at telling Diana my news, I don't have any recollection of what I said to my parents. My father was so uninvolved in my life that my absence wasn't going to affect him much; when my sisters presented the plan to him as a fait accompli, he had no objections. What about my mother? Did Robin explain that I was going to leave? I can't be certain. And although I know I should be able to find a memory of my mother the day I left, it's a blank. My mother was forty-six years old and watching her youngest child leave home. Her marriage was over; her nest was empty. But as hard as I try, I can't picture her face as we said good-bye. Perhaps I was so focused on looking ahead of me that I forgot to turn and look back.

What I do know is that my mother didn't at any point try to stand in my way. She let me go. I think she knew in her heart that she didn't have the strength to take care of me anymore, and in her own way, she wanted to do what was right for me. If I went to live with my sister, it would be one less struggle for her to bear, and maybe I would have a chance at a better life.

THAT OCTOBER, I started my new life in New York. Jill was twenty-three years old and living in a small studio apartment at Thirty-third and Third Avenue. She'd begun working as a booking agent at the Wilhelmina modeling agency, crossing paths with famous models of the day such as Margaux Hemingway and Pam Dawber. I started at the Rhodes School, a small private school on West Fifty-fourth Street between Fifth and Sixth Avenues. Rhodes wasn't at all elite or academic, and even with my less than perfect school records, I was able to pass the entrance exam. The fees must have been somewhat affordable as well, as my father paid for them using the money that Sherman had left in his will for my education.

Now that I'd left home, my parents rented out the house on Long Island and began divorce proceedings. My mother went to live with Robin in Philadelphia, while my father moved to Manhattan. He found a fourth-floor apartment in a brownstone on Fifty-third Street near Fifth Avenue, and, soon after, Jill and I moved into a fourth-floor walkup just across the street. The apartment didn't have a kitchen and needed a lot of work, but we were eager to leave Jill's tiny studio, and the rent was cheaper on Fifty-third. Our new apartment had long dark wooden beams crossing the ceiling and an old fireplace that no longer worked. Jill and I refinished the floors and painted the walls with a stucco effect. My father built a small bar to give us a kitchen area, and we bought a refrigerator, toaster oven, and hot plate. There was one bedroom, where Jill and I slept on mattresses on the floor. Malcolm paid my share of the rent and, in the beginning at least, gave me sixty dollars a month for food.

From the minute I arrived, I loved New York. For the first time in my life, I felt free to come and go as I pleased. Each day, I walked to school along Fifth Avenue, a distance of exactly one block. Right below the apartment, there was a little hamburger place where I'd stop for a burger whenever I had the money. On the weekends, Jill and I often went out together. She'd take me to the nearby Hilton Hotel for drinks with her friends; then we'd go to a disco where they didn't check IDs, where we could order white wine spritzers and dance the Hustle. Everyone in Jill's group was kind to me, the little sister. When we had money to spare, which wasn't often, we'd go downtown to Orchard Street or the Village, where Jill's model friends told us we could get great deals. I remember buying blue bell-bottom jeans at the new Fiorucci emporium after it opened, right around the corner from Bloomingdale's.

I was learning on my feet, racing to educate myself, to grow up, all the time trying to leave my childhood behind me. Away from my mother, I never missed a day of school. I loved Rhodes and was eager to make up for lost time. My lack of education had taught me to listen carefully, to follow others, to learn by emulating what I saw around me. By the end of the year, I was getting straight A's in Spanish, social studies, algebra—nearly all of my classes. I even made the honor roll. I wanted to succeed. I didn't want to miss out on anything. I would have gone to school with a 102-degree fever if that was what it took. After school, I did my homework. Jill bought a vocabulary-building book—*30 Days to a More Powerful Vocabulary*—and we would read it together. I remember looking in the book and learning the meaning of the word "altruism": "the unselfish regard for or devotion to the welfare of others." This made such an impression on me: that a whole philosophy of life could be contained in a single word.

In my rush to escape from my parents and their influence, I attached myself to anyone who could give me the stability and structure that they'd been unable to provide. Chendo Perez was a grade ahead of me at the Rhodes School. He was tall and good-looking, with dark eyes and wavy brown hair. We connected with a teenage intensity that convinced both of us we'd be together forever.

Chendo's family lived in a small house in Queens with a tiny kitchen that was the hub of the home—the place where the entire family gathered, talking over one another in Spanish, making food, breaking bread. Chendo was born in Cuba, where his parents had been wealthy jewelers, but when Fidel Castro came to power, they were forced to leave. Now his father ran a jewelry business on Forty-seventh Street in the Diamond District, while his mother stayed home to take care of the family. There was no tension between Chendo's parents, just a sense of pride for the life they had built together in a new land. Marina, the mother, had a kind of fierce love for her three children. She was so connected to her son and two daughters, always talking, hugging, encouraging, laughing with them; this was the complete opposite of my own silent, withdrawn, and withholding mother. I had never learned how to cook, so Marina taught me how to make picadillo (a Cuban dish made from ground beef, onions, and peppers) and frijoles negros (black beans) and rice in a pressure cooker. Chendo's sisters, Marina and Marta, were so young and innocent, guided and protected by their strict parents, something I had never experienced in my own childhood. The Perez family embraced me, took care of me, and showed me what a happy, functioning family looks like. Yes, I'd fallen in love with Chendo, but I loved his family, too.

I slipped happily into the role of surrogate daughter and sister.

MY MOTHER STAYED in Philadelphia for some months after leaving the house on Long Island. Then, toward the end of my first year at the Rhodes School, she moved to Manhattan, to an apartment in the Seventies on the Upper East Side. The apartment had barely any furniture, but what little furniture there was, my mother kept covered in white sheets or plastic wrap. She had developed a terrible fear of germs; she needed everything around her to be white and pure, including her clothing. When I visited, I had to make sure to wash my hands before touching anything.

After she moved to the city, I confess, I didn't see my mother all that much. The more time I spent away from her, the more I began to realize that Robin had been right. I *hadn't* been sick. I *didn't* have internal bleeding or a weak heart. I didn't have tuberculosis or rheumatic fever or pneumonia either. There was nothing I needed to be "cured" of in Lourdes. My mother had kept me home all those years without any valid reason. Away from her, I did well in school, doing my best to move on from my childhood in order to survive.

When I turned sixteen in November, Jill threw a surprise sweet sixteen party for me at our apartment. Both my parents came. Robin traveled in from Philadelphia. My half sister, Patricia, Chendo, and a few of our friends from the Rhodes School were there. I remember I wore a floral skirt and dusty-rose-colored scoop-neck shirt, my hair parted in the middle and ironed flat so that it swung at my shoulders. It was a wonderful night for me. I remember how important it felt that my sisters and I were together as family. We had survived the divorce and leaving the house on Long Island. We were adjusting. I felt buoyed up by the support of the people who cared about me. At some point in the evening, someone took a photograph of my father with his four daughters—the only one that was ever taken. My mother wasn't in the picture. She sat in one spot for most of the night, not saying a word.

It was not long after my sixteenth birthday that my father announced he had run out of money. He told me that he could no longer afford to pay for my tuition and that I was going to have to leave the

Rhodes School. I was finally experiencing educational success, and now it was being taken away from me. I was heartbroken.

I went with my mother to visit the local public school, but all I remember is the yellow-tile walls covered in graffiti and being terrified of such a big school and so many students.

At the same time, Chendo had been offered a job on the Caribbean island of St. Thomas, managing a jewelry store for a family friend. He wanted me to go with him. His new employers promised me a job as a counter manager for Clinique in the same store. The choice was so simple: my boyfriend and I were in love, and I wanted to make my life with him. His family wanted me to go with him to St. Thomas. So I decided that was what I was going to do.

Chendo and I decided we needed to see my mother to tell her about our plans.

"Well, at least that's one I don't have to worry about" were her words.

I was sixteen, already living apart from her, and now I was moving with my boyfriend 1,600 miles away. But my mother didn't stand in my way. The following week, she took me to an ob-gyn, staying in the room with me as the doctor fitted me for a diaphragm.

That August, Chendo and I flew to St. Thomas, moving into an apartment complex on a hilltop overlooking the city. Once I arrived on the island, I sent my father a letter to say I was going to St. Thomas to get "a different kind of education."

Years later, I learned the real reason I had to leave the Rhodes School. My father had decided to write a novel. He'd used the funds that Sherman had left me for my education to pay for his trip to Europe for his research.

ON ST. THOMAS, I started working full-time as a cosmetics counter manager in a department store, C. & M. Caron. I enjoyed the job, getting dressed up every morning, helping my customers, having the responsibility of handling sales. After work, Chendo and I played at being grown-ups. I bought a Betty Crocker cookbook called *Cooking for Two* and started to try my hand at cooking. One of the first dishes I tried was meatballs. They turned out square. Chendo thought this was hilarious.

On my days off, I'd sip piña coladas on a raft at the pool attached to our apartment building, or Chendo and I would take the ferry over to Trunk Bay to go snorkeling. I was scared to snorkel at first. I'd never taken a swimming lesson in my life, and I could barely doggy-paddle. But Chendo encouraged me and made me feel safe, until I was completely at ease in the water. The island was surrounded by miles of coral reefs and hidden coves. Underwater, I saw every kind of brightly colored fish and coral, turtle, ray, and sponge in magical formations. Paddling through the turquoise water, I was transported to a world of stunning beauty and peace.

My new salary gave me choices and the ability to pursue my own tastes and interests. I began to wear designer clothes and silk blouses with the gold jewelry that Chendo had given to me. I remember I bought a crystal statue of the Greek god and goddess Pan and Diana, made by Lalique, because I was fascinated with Greek mythology. I started going to calisthenics classes, trying to make up for all the years my mother had made sure I was excused from gym. Chendo and I moved to a bigger apartment at Sapphire Bay Resort, a much nicer complex on the other end of the island with views of the ocean from our terrace. Now that we had more space, I rented an upright piano for ten dollars a month. I had wanted to play piano ever since I was old enough to beg for lessons, the only thing I remember fighting for as a child. My mother had arranged for lessons for me but they didn't last. Before long my parents announced they couldn't afford to pay for them anymore.

Now that I had my own money, I found a piano teacher who lived close by. She was a petite woman in her sixties with white-blond hair and skin that was tan and leathery from years under the island sun. She was kind, patient, and motherly, and I practiced for hours each day hoping to win her approval and make her proud. I played Beethoven's "Für Elise" over and over, sensing the emotion written into the music as the notes escalated, then quieted again. I learned to play Tchaikovsky's melodies for *The Nutcracker*, all the music my mother and I loved from our trips to the ballet. I pounded and caressed the keys until I improved, and I felt real pride in my skill. It was as if I had finally found the structure and discipline my parents had failed to offer me growing up. Playing piano gave me something else I had never experienced before: a sense of accomplishment.

The following year, Chendo and I were married. I was only seventeen, and he was nineteen. We went to the courthouse and filled out the paperwork. I wore a matching Courrèges shirt and skirt with a white, turquoise, and pink pattern. Chendo wore his best pair of pants and a short sleeved button-down shirt. When the judge pronounced us husband and wife, there was a moment of hesitation between us. We were so young; I don't think either of us had ever attended a wedding before. Was this the part where we were supposed to kiss? The judge looked at us and laughed, saying, "You may kiss the bride!" Afterward, we went to the nearby island of St. Barts for our honeymoon.

As Chendo and I neared our second Christmas on the island, I began talking with Robin about bringing our mother to visit. I was a married woman now, completely emancipated from my family, but even so, I wanted to share some of my happiness with them. I knew that my mother hadn't been doing well. Jill had found her a job at a small store, but it was more than she could manage, and the owner let her go. Robin arranged the travel plans and booked and paid for the flights. I met them at the airport. I noticed right away how different my mother looked. Her hair was longer than she liked, falling around her shoulders, and under the bright skies of the islands, she seemed frail and out of place.

Even so, I was eager to show my mother and sister my new life. One of my favorite recipes from my Betty Crocker *Cooking for Two* cookbook was Cornish hens, served with wild rice and homemade cranberry sauce in orange cups. The night they arrived, I made it for the four of us, setting the table carefully, hoping my mother would notice my care. Chendo and I had bought a Christmas tree and set it up next to my piano. That night, I put on my favorite floral dress with a black velvet bodice. After I served dinner, I sat at the piano next to the tree and played for my mother and sister. I had worked tirelessly to perfect Chopin's Waltz no. 7, which I knew was featured in one of my mother's favorite films, *The Red Shoes*.

I wanted to share everything that I loved about my new life with both of them, especially my mother. I wanted her to see that I had escaped from our cycle of sickness and absence, and that I was thriving.

During their stay, Robin and my mother took the short walk with me down to the beach—two miles of soft white sand and clear blue waters that met a bright blue sky at the horizon. I was going to show my mother and sister how to snorkel.

We waded into the warm, shallow water, and I helped my mother put on her snorkel mask, tightening the straps and adjusting the breathing tube. I remember she was wearing a swimsuit in pale pink, always her favorite color. I explained how she was going to float on top of the water and submerge her face, breathing through the tube in her mouth. I wanted her to practice now because in a day or so we were planning to go by ferry to Trunk Bay, the best place for snorkeling in the area.

My mother watched me as I demonstrated what to do, and then, awkwardly, she bent down and put her face to the water, just barely beneath the surface. Immediately, she stood up again, gasping. I encouraged her to try one more time. It really wasn't that complicated. Again she put her face to the water, then stood right back up again. I felt immediately annoyed. This shouldn't be a big deal. It was so simple for me, and I had never even taken swimming lessons because she had always been too worried I would catch a cold. If I could do it, anyone could! I begged her to just try, told her that there was a whole magical world beneath us—the darting yellow and orange fish, the magnificent flame-colored coral. I wanted to share it with her; I hoped it would make her happy, the same way it made *me* happy. But instead, she just stood there, staring up at me, her wet pink bathing suit clinging to her thin frame, the mask on her face making her look like a lost child.

At that instant, I couldn't stand it anymore.

For the first time in my life, I allowed myself to become furious with my mother.

"All I wanted was for you to experience this one thing," I told her, tears forming in my eyes. "You're not even *trying!*"

It was so rare for me to show my feelings to anyone. That was something that Robin did, or Jill at times, but not me. I was too intent on being "the good one"—always quiet and obedient, watchful of others and considerate of *their* feelings. But I couldn't hold back *my* feelings a moment longer.

"Why can't you do anything I need you to do?" I bawled at her. "What is wrong with you?"

Years of pent-up anger and hurt came spilling out.

"Why is it up to *me* to teach you how to do this anyway?" I asked. "Why aren't *you* teaching me something for a change?"

Even in the moment, I knew my tantrum was selfish. It was silly, over nothing. But I couldn't control it. My mother was incapable of giving me what I needed as her daughter. She just stood in the water, trembling, looking down at the waves, her mask hanging uselessly around her neck, the tube of the snorkel drooping.

"I'm so sorry," she kept repeating, shaking her head. "It's my fault."

The fact that she blamed herself infuriated me even more. She never took a stand. She always backed down, blaming herself, even with my father! That she was unable to defend herself against my pathetic attack was the final indignity. No wonder my sisters always described her as "the martyr." I stalked away, leaving Robin to pick up the pieces.

Back at the apartment, I sat down in the living room, looking around me. I had my rented piano and my cookbook for two; I had my husband, my little crystal statue, my job at the department store, my clothes in my closet. I was seventeen years old, and this was my world, and I had made it myself. I wasn't going to be silent anymore. I alone was in charge of my own destiny.

Later that week, my mother and Robin went home. I stayed on the island for the next two years, living completely independently from my family. Although Robin came to visit me again while I was there, my mother never did.

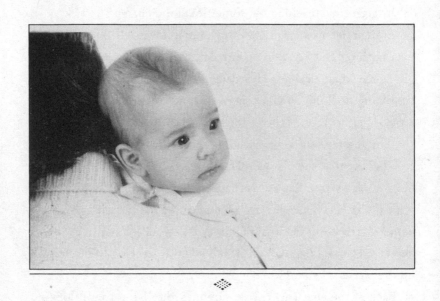

CHAPTER 15

Carolyn

It was Fred, Sherman's groundskeeper, who came to the hospital to pick up my mother and me to bring us home that cold day in late November. Fred helped Carolyn to the car, holding her arm so she wouldn't slip. He was always kindly that way. Together, we returned to the Dream House. In the weeks to come, the snow continued to fall, until there were fourteen inches of white covering the land. The nanny took Jill and Robin to the school bus each day and brought them home in the afternoon while Carolyn rested and tried to get her strength back. It was months before the incision fully healed and she felt as if she could move around easily. During the week, Malcolm was in the city for work. He was uninterested in the baby and Carolyn's recovery, which seemed to bore him. On the weekends, he disappeared next door to Sherman's parties, his busy social life continuing more or less unchanged.

The first time my mother left the house with me, it was so cold she had to bundle me up in coats and blankets to protect me from the artic wind coming in from the frozen Sound. "Long Island in winter is like living in a Russian novel," she used to say.

Grace wrote letters regularly, keeping Carolyn updated on the children's progress, her official duties, and life at the palace. But it was hard for Carolyn to write back. What could she say? That she was unhappy living out at the end of the world? That the older children made so much noise and were so demanding, and that the baby often refused to settle, leaving her feeling helpless? That her career as a model was over? That her body had been destroyed by the three surgeries? That ever since the hysterectomy she was getting hot flashes, going through menopause at age thirty? That she didn't want Malcolm anywhere near her? Next door, at Sherman's castle, a regular parade of young models arrived each weekend. As she waited for her husband to come home at night, she knew she had been replaced. The more difficult her life became, the less Carolyn felt herself worthy of her friendship with Grace, the unimpeachable princess.

Every now and again, Malcolm would invite their friends from the city out to the new house for parties. Eileen Ford and her husband, Jerry, came to visit. Hope Lange, a young actress they had both known from Manhattan House days, would also drop by, and Tippi Hedren, one of my mother's modeling friends, would come to stay for the weekend. But Carolyn no longer felt at ease in social situations. She was too awkward now, out of place, as if she were always about to say or do the wrong thing. She could no longer rely on her youth or prettiness. It didn't help that when Malcolm told jokes and stories, they were usually at her expense. On the rare occasion she met someone new, either through the children or Malcolm, she never knew quite where she stood. People seemed to automatically know that she was the bridesmaid—after all, Grace's wedding had been televised around the world in front of thirty million viewers—but Carolyn was never sure if they really wanted to be her friend or if they were just fascinated by her connection to the princess.

She had assumed that after the wedding, Grace would vanish from her life, but that hadn't been the case. Grace was determined to keep up with her old friends, and to find ways of including them in her new life. Before my birth, my mother had written to Grace in Monaco, asking for a favor. My mother had a cousin from Steubenville, Sandra. They had grown up next door to each other, and even though my mother was ten years older than Sandra, they had remained close. Sandra was in high school and had decided she wanted to study to be an actress at the American Academy of Dramatic Arts, Grace's former acting school. However, Sandra couldn't afford to travel back and forth to New York for the auditions, which took place in the spring, and—should she get a place—buy another ticket when classes started in September. Carolyn wrote to Grace, explaining the situation; my mother knew that Grace would do whatever she could to help a young woman with dreams of a career in the arts. Grace wrote to the American Academy of Dramatic Arts, asking if Sandra could audition in September, so she would only have to pay for one ticket to New York. The Academy agreed. In the end, Sandra's father didn't allow her to go to the audition—he didn't approve of Sandra's becoming an actress. But by the time I was born, Sandra had finally gotten permission to move to Manhattan to study to be a secretary at the Katherine Gibbs School.

The year of my birth, Sandra moved to New York. She was nineteen years old and staying at the Barbizon Hotel in New York, just as Grace and Carolyn had done. The next spring, when I was six months old, Carolyn received word that Grace was going to come to visit us at the Dream House, so she invited Sandra to join us. I was too young to remember the visit, but years later Sandra recounted it for me. While the royal security detail waited outside in the limousine, Her Serene Highness Princess Grace bustled into our home, bringing gifts for me and for Jill and Robin. Grace looked as beautiful as ever, her hair pulled back, her skin the color of porcelain; Carolyn led her friend and Sandra to the living room, so they could sit comfortably. Grace was wearing expensive leather shoes with a tiny heel, which she slipped off. She curled up her legs on the couch, enjoying the warmth from the fireplace (the palace in Monaco was notoriously cold).

Together, Carolyn and Grace reminisced about the past. Carolyn went to dig out *The Pursuit of Destiny*, the book of horoscopes they'd loved to read to one another during evenings at the Manhattan House. They found the familiar pages containing their fortunes and began to read. The future once foretold in the pages had become the present. Grace had fulfilled her destiny, "taking center of any stage, as by divine right, and occupying it successfully, with popularity and charm." Carolyn's fortune had always been much more mixed. The book had warned her that she would end up here, her energies scattered, her mental balance gone. "Irritable, nervous and undependable" were the words the horoscope used to describe her fate. Sandra was still at the beginning of her journey. Her horoscope promised that she had "constructive energy, creative ability, courage and dependability," and that she would be able to "accomplish anything—within reason."

Later that afternoon, Grace left in her limousine, and Sandra took the train into the city. Carolyn was alone with the children. Outside the windows of the Dream House, the sun set over the inlet and the muddy beach. Now that Grace and Sandra were gone, there was nothing to distract Carolyn from her absent husband, the children that didn't listen, the baby that cried too loudly and for too long. Carolyn was at land's end, on the edge of the woods. There were days she didn't know if she could get up in the morning to feed the children breakfast. Other days, she couldn't stop, with so much energy she didn't sleep at night; she just kept going, her mind refusing to shut down. She knew now that all the elements—people, places, things, the movement of the planets overhead—were connected. She alone could understand this. She heard noises everywhere, and she knew what they meant. The creakings and knockings in the house's tall wooden walls. The rustling of the swallows under the eaves, like voices whispering; the fox that came up to the window and stared inside at her, its eyes flashing. They were sending her messages. She had to stay alert. It was up to her to listen.

Carolyn knew that something was wrong. She wasn't herself. She made an appointment to see a psychiatrist in Manhattan, a Dr. Green.

Soon she was driving into the city each week for the sessions. She didn't tell Malcolm; she knew he would only disapprove. Eventually, Malcolm discovered the check stubs. He confronted Carolyn. He was furious. Why was she wasting his money on city doctors? When she explained she had been seeing a psychiatrist, Malcolm demanded she switch to a doctor of his choosing, and he made it a condition of him paying for further treatment. But Carolyn kept going to Dr. Green, until Malcolm found the check stubs again and put a stop to the visits once and for all.

THE FOLLOWING YEAR, Princess Grace telephoned my mother at the house on Long Island. She was coming to New York at the end of April, bringing her children with her to visit America for the first time. They would be in the city for only a few days before traveling on to Philadelphia; Prince Rainier would be joining them there. Grace wanted to make a date to take her old friend and her goddaughter Jill to the ballet. Grace would bring Princess Caroline along—now four years old.

They agreed on a date to meet and that they would go to see the New York City Ballet at City Center. It would be just like old times. My mother bought Jill a new party dress and tied a big bow in her hair for the occasion. Jill was ten. I was barely two years old; that day I stayed at home with our babysitter and Robin.

As Carolyn waited in the lobby of City Center with Jill, she was reminded of all the times she had come here with Grace in their Barbizon days, lured here by the beauty of the dancers and Balanchine's choreography. At eighteen and nineteen years old, things were so easy between them. The currents of their lives ran in the same direction, flowing only forward, out through the revolving doors of the Barbizon and into the world. They were women with a shared past now; there were secrets between them. Carolyn was thirty-two; Grace was thirty-one. Carolyn had her three children, Grace her two. They would never again be those young girls, in love with the city, with the ballet, with the beautiful unknown future. The currents of their lives no longer ran in the same direction, and Carolyn knew she wasn't going to be able to fall back into the flow.

The princess arrived, holding little Caroline's hand. Grace hugged her friend, hugged Jill, who had grown so tall since the last time they had seen each other. Grace was radiant, warm, but controlled. Carolyn was so impressed by the way Grace handed Caroline, still only four years old, the money to buy her own program, and by the way the little princess counted out the change using the unfamiliar American coins. The two mothers and their daughters entered the theater, taking their seats in the orchestra, a few seats back from the stage. At this point, the entire house began to applaud, and Grace turned around and waved regally. Carolyn wondered how it must feel: to be so completely admired.

The ballet was *Swan Lake,* and in Balanchine's version, the story was distilled into a single act. Tchaikovsky's sweet, sad music began to play. As the curtain came up, the stage was dimly lit, a glittering lake in the background. Hunters carrying crossbows appeared, but as the music continued to build, the hunters exited the stage, leaving Prince Siegfried alone to watch the Swan Queen, Odette, arrive onstage. Together the Prince and Queen danced, Siegfried lifting her high into the air. Toward the end of the scene, Von Rothbart, the cruel sorcerer who cast the swan spell on Odette, appeared in his cape and mask—and Odette ran away.

Next, the swans floated in, wearing their white tutus, forming a dramatic long diagonal line across the stage, then peeling off, one after the other, as Siegfried passed them. They danced with each other and with the hunters, in a constantly changing spectacle of pattern and movement. Odette danced alone and with her lover. Siegfried danced alone and with Odette. The swans returned, in groups and in their full numbers. Finally, Von Rothbart appeared again, commanding the swans to leave. Odette went with them, beating her arms like sorrowful wings. Siegfried and the hunters were left alone, heads bowed. The curtain fell. In the space of one act, Balanchine had told the story of doomed love, from beginning all the way to bitter end.

As far as I can tell, the trip to the ballet was the last time Grace and Carolyn were together. In the years to come, they corresponded, but I have no record of them ever meeting again. After her visit, Grace returned to Monaco, to her palace, her husband, and her royal duties. My mother retreated, back to Long Island and her isolation.

CHAPTER 16

Nina

In 1978, after three years on St. Thomas, Chendo and I moved back to New York. The island had been a perfect getaway, but both Chendo and I knew it couldn't last forever. We missed our families, and I missed living in a big city. We decided to come home. My husband went to work for his father's jewelry business, and I found a job at Bergdorf Goodman's department store at the Clinique cosmetics counter. We bought a small co-op apartment together in Queens, not far from his parents.

While we had been gone, the Dream House on Long Island had been sold, but for far less money than my parents had hoped. While they had been waiting for the divorce to come through, they had rented out the place, but the renters had neglected to take care of the property, and the house had fallen into disrepair. Cabinets had been ripped out of the walls, doors were hanging on hinges, and the bathtubs were coated with rust. The garden had grown over, my father's beloved marigold beds were filled with weeds, and there were beer cans strewn around the property. For a time, the Dream House stood abandoned altogether, the neighborhood kids using the yard as a passageway to tramp down to the beach.

After the sale of the house was completed, my father and mother took an equal share from the proceeds. My mother had been living in Philadelphia with Robin. Now she was able to move into an apartment in Manhattan on West Fifty-eighth Street.

This was where she was living the night of January 28, 1979, the night my father knocked on her door late, wearing a black suit.

He had come to tell her the news from which my mother—in fact, all of us—would never recover. Robin was dead.

That night, my sister had gone on a date. The guy owned a brandnew yellow Corvette. He was driving Robin home. He lost control of the car, hitting a bridge abutment. He survived, but no one could save Robin. When the paramedics reached the scene of the accident, "Stairway to Heaven" was playing on the car radio.

Chendo was the one to tell me. We were staying at his parents' house in Queens. I remember I fell to the floor; I lay there in a fetal position, holding myself as the sobs racked my body. Chendo's little sisters came into the room. I remember they were staring down at me; I knew I was scaring them, but there was nothing I could do. I felt like I couldn't breathe; how would I ever live in a world without her?

A week later, our family came together in Philadelphia for Robin's funeral. My mother, Jill, Patricia, and I gathered around Robin's open casket to say our good-byes. We were all distraught, my mother silent, her eyes hollow with pain, the powder on her face streaked with tears. My sister's beautiful face was expressionless, painted with the thick mortician's makeup. She was wearing the long-sleeved navy-blue dress with a white collar that my mother had picked out for her. I remember my mother leaned down into the coffin and tenderly moved Robin's legs, one away from the other, before she went to her grave. A mother's final gesture of care.

After we said our good-byes, I turned to my mother and sisters and asked that we make a pact to be close. We had been through so much—illness, divorce, tragedy—but it was clear to me that Robin would want us to come together now, to move forward as a united front. I hoped we could, for her.

My father was also at the funeral. I had never seen him so upset. His relationship with Robin had always been tumultuous, but after years of estrangement, they had recently reconnected. My father had gone to see one of Robin's concerts, and my sister had taken it as a sign that they could move forward. The church that day was full of Robin's friends; so many people had wanted to come to pay their respects. Patricia, Jill, and I stood up in the front and read the lyrics from one of Robin's songs, "Lady in Waiting." "You'll still guide my hand, through a world that I don't understand," Robin had written, "and you'll still protect me from the pain, when you're gone. Oh when you're gone, I will remain."

Robin's loss was more than any of us could bear, but it completely devastated our mother. Of her three daughters, Robin was the one who could make my mother laugh, who could actually put her at ease. When my mother and Robin talked, they had long conversations where my mother actually opened up and shared what was in her heart. Robin had always been so confident and calm, and even Robin couldn't be saved. Robin's death marked the point my mother gave up; the rest of her life became a kind of endurance.

After Robin died, I completely shut down. Robin was the only person I ever really trusted in my family to tell me the truth and to support me. I blamed myself completely for her death. I had planned to visit my sister that weekend of her death, but at the last minute I had canceled. If I'd been with her, she never would have gone out on the date. She might still be here with us.

My relationship with Chendo suffered. We couldn't agree on where to live. I wanted to be in Manhattan, not in Queens, but his parents wanted us close by. We were still so young, barely out of our teens, and the pressure of marriage and buying a home was too much for us. Chendo wanted to make it work, but I had nothing left to give. We signed a legal separation in July 1980. After that, we sold our co-op, and I moved into an apartment on Seventy-seventh near Third Avenue. I was just twenty.

I remember that after my marriage to Chendo ended, my mother went with me to a furniture store in the city to help me pick out a pullout couch. It was blue with a delicate flower pattern, the kind of fabric that she loved. For once, we found something we could agree on, as I loved the couch, too. I remember feeling so happy she was showing an interest in my life that when she offered to pay for the couch, I agreed.

If I had known how little money she had, I never would have let her. It was only much later I learned that her nest egg from the sale of the Long Island house was almost gone. She had handed her share of the money over to an investment broker at Merrill Lynch. My mother knew nothing about finance, and the broker took full advantage. He churned the stock to generate commissions, until her account was whittled away to almost nothing. The little money she did have left she started giving away to the TV evangelists she watched on her black-and-white set in her apartment. I remember going to visit her and finding a slim stack of envelopes on the credenza, each envelope holding a single dollar bill and addressed to an evangelist. She called these donations "tithing."

While my mother withdrew inside herself, my grief after Robin's death propelled me forward. Right before she died, Robin was beginning to make a name for herself as a singer-songwriter, playing the clubs and bars of Philadelphia. She had always been musical. A scout from Warner Bros. had spotted her, and she was in talks for a record deal. Robin hadn't lived long enough to achieve her dream, but I became determined to achieve some of mine. I got my GED, finally able to say I was a high school graduate. I began to think about a career beyond working at Bergdorf's. I knew I was tall and slender and photographed well. I had had some modeling test shots taken, borrowing my mother's pale yellow bridesmaid's dress from Grace's wedding to wear for the shoot.

(Later that year, with complete disregard for the dress and its historical value, I wore it to a Halloween party at the Underground

Club in New York. I don't remember what happened to the dress after that. Somewhere along the way, with so many of my mother's other belongings, it was lost.)

I connected with some of the smaller modeling agencies and did more test shots. I started to have some success, and my portfolio grew. I left Bergdorf's to focus on my new career. I met with my mother's agent, Eileen Ford. She remembered my mother well and wanted to help, but she told me I was better suited for runway than for print. She sent me to Gillis MacGill, the owner of the Mannequin modeling agency. Gillis was in the process of putting together a group of girls to send to Japan, and I was given a three-month contract. All I needed was the plane fare. My father loaned me a thousand dollars for the flight. Everything else would be taken care of when we got there—the agency in Tokyo would handle our living arrangements. I stayed in Japan for five months, appearing in TV commercials, print ads, and runway shows.

Now that I was modeling seriously, I changed my name from Nina to Nyna with a *y*, to help me stand out. My sister Jill had already changed her name to Jyl with a *y*. I kept hurtling forward in life, pulling together whatever pieces I felt I needed to make a complete picture for myself as I went.

Then I met David. I was on the plane traveling to Tokyo. He was heading there on business. I remember he was goofing around with some children on the airplane, entertaining them during the long flight. From the first moment I felt drawn to him, to his strength and kindness. After we both returned to the States, we became inseparable. He was so supportive, offering me the kind of stability I knew I needed. Soon after, we decided to get married, and a year and a half later, I was pregnant. My new husband was everything I felt I wanted and needed. He came from such a good family, and his mother, Dee Dee, was a wonderful, loving person, too. My new mother-in-law had two sons; she started referring to me as the daughter she never had. Dee Dee and I went shopping together and met for lunches at Bloomingdale's. These were small things, but they meant the world to me. Like Chendo's mother before her, she became my surrogate mother.

While I had been away in Japan, my own mother had lost the apartment on Fifty-eighth Street. She moved to Philadelphia, as if she could somehow feel closer to Robin there. Jyl was also living in Philadelphia by then. We were both so worried about our mother. Housing was a continual problem; our mother was always bouncing from place to place. For a short time, she lived at a home for women run by Catholic nuns just outside Philadelphia. None of us understood or knew what to do. In August 1982, Jyl decided to call Grace in Monaco. Grace had sent such a kind condolence note to my mother after Robin died; perhaps she would have some advice for us now. Jyl managed to reach Grace at the palace. The princess promised Jyl she would do anything she could to help. She was planning to come to New York later in September. Perhaps she could see Carolyn then.

But Grace never returned to New York. That September, she was driving her daughter Stephanie to the train station in Monaco when she lost control of her car on the coastal road, crashing through a retaining wall and onto the rocky slopes below. The night before the news broke, my mother had dreamt of two figures tumbling and falling, one of them a small child in pink, the other a larger figure, holding the child's hand.

The funeral was held in the same cathedral where Grace had married Prince Rainier, where my mother had stood by her side as a bridesmaid all those years ago. The other members of Grace's retinue were there to say good-bye, but my mother did not attend the service. By then, she had moved so many times that no one at the palace knew how to contact her to send her an invitation. Even if they had, my mother had neither the strength nor the means to travel.

GRACE'S DEATH, coming so soon after Robin's, was more than my mother's fragile health could withstand. She moved into yet another apartment in Philadelphia, this one in the projects, in a very bad area. I remember going to visit her there. It was winter, and even inside the temperature was frigid. There was no bedroom or separate kitchen in the apartment. I noticed that my mother had put a pack of American cheese on the window ledge. Why would she have put it there? Was it to keep it cool because she didn't have power? Could she pay her bills? I didn't ask. She was so gaunt—her hair was streaked with silver; she couldn't afford to color it anymore.

That day, I kept my coat on throughout my visit.

I was four months pregnant and just starting to show. I didn't want her to see, to know that I was going to be a mother. I felt such an intense need to protect my unborn child from her influence, to do things my own way. I stayed for about an hour. Then I left. Looking back, it breaks my heart that I could just leave her there. I was twenty-three. I didn't know how to help her; I didn't know what else to do.

MY DAUGHTER WAS BORN via C-section, just as I had been born. I promised her I was going to do whatever it took to give her the childhood I'd lacked. I read Nicole baby books, I played with her, I adored her.

David and I had moved to an apartment in the suburbs. I gave up working to devote myself to motherhood, to building my normal life.

It was here at the apartment that I got the call from a doctor at Kings County Psychiatric Hospital in Brooklyn.

"I am calling about your mother," the doctor said.

What was my mother doing in New York? She was supposed to be in Philadelphia. I remember sitting down, preparing for the worst. Nicole was playing on the carpet in the living room, wearing a little pink dress, the light streaming in through the living room windows.

The doctor explained that my mother had been brought to the hospital babbling and incoherent. Somehow, she had managed to give the doctor my number.

"What's wrong with her?" I asked, terrified.

"You don't know?" he asked, sounding surprised. "It seems to us that she has paranoid schizophrenia."

I knew that my mother was in trouble. I knew that she was struggling. I knew there was something very wrong. But until now, no one had ever mentioned schizophrenia or a diagnosis of mental illness of any kind. I had no understanding of the disease; I just knew that I needed to do whatever I could to help her.

The doctor explained they weren't going to be able to commit my mother. To keep her at the psychiatric hospital, she would have to be a danger to herself or someone else. Instead, they were going to send her to a place where she could be treated, where she would be safe. There was a shelter for mentally ill women age fifty-five and over on the Upper East Side. This would be a stepping-stone to housing, a temporary measure. The staff here would be able to get her the help, services, and treatment she needed.

This was how my mother found herself at the shelter at the old Park Avenue Armory on the Upper East Side.

At the shelter, my mother refused to take any medication. The staff tried to arrange for housing; she wouldn't participate in the process. She felt she couldn't trust them. In the coming months, everyone who knew her tried to persuade her to move. My grandmother in Ohio wanted her to come back to Steubenville and live with her there. There was a cousin in Steubenville who offered her a room. Another relative in Florida was going to lend her a condo rent-free until she got on her feet. I tried to persuade her to come to the suburbs near me, so we could be close. But she turned everyone down.

It was a devastating time for everyone who loved my mother. No one could understand why she wouldn't comply with the staff and why she turned down our offers of help. It was never explained to us that this behavior was in keeping with her diagnosis; that those who are the most seriously mentally ill don't realize that they are sick, so they often won't accept help and treatment. It was only years later that I learned that her obstinacy was actually another symptom of her illness, that what my mother really needed was an advocate, someone to take charge of her life and intervene at every level. I was so completely uneducated about the causes and effects of mental illness. I simply didn't have the tools I needed to be that person on her behalf.

I was also preoccupied. I was nearly thirty, the mother of two now; my son, Michael, had just been born. It was during this period that my daughter, Nicole, began to suffer with seizures. The first time it happened, she was two and a half years old, and I was with her and the new baby at the grocery store. Suddenly, Nicole started gripping the cart, staring straight ahead. Her body was rigid; her mouth was opening and closing. I asked her if she was okay, but she didn't respond; she didn't even seem to recognize me. I rushed her to the pediatrician. The pediatrician sent me to a neurologist. Nicole had a seizure right there in the doctor's office.

We were told she had a seizure disorder and needed to go on medication—but the medication didn't work.

No one seemed to know how to help her. We tried everything: different medications, diets, specialists, hospitals. After what I had been through as a child, it was almost more than I could bear. I was the daughter of a mother who had kept me home mistakenly believing I was sick. Now I was the parent of a child who had a *legitimate* health concern, and no one knew how to help us. We were in and out of clinics and hospitals. My ob-gyn told me I was going through "every parent's worst nightmare." Through it all, I refused to let my daughter stay home from school. I needed her to get an education. I couldn't let her miss out as I had done.

OVER TIME, MY MOTHER established a routine for herself at the shelter, one that she followed religiously. In the morning, she got up and got dressed, always in white. Then she went to Bergdorf Goodman's to wash in the basins of the ladies' room. If it rained or if it was cold, she visited the Performing Arts Library at Lincoln Center, where she could listen to classical ballet music on headphones, the same symphonies she had played for me as a child. She had a watercolor set, and she liked to sit on a bench and paint pictures of flowers and animals. She went to church often, taking her place in one of the pews and listening to the sermon, or praying in front of a statue of her beloved Virgin Mary. And every single day, with ritualistic intensity, she went to the little park set in between the buildings on Fifty-eighth Street to pray. She believed the park was blessed, and that if she went there often enough, miracles would come to pass. She felt that her prayers would someday elevate the park to the level of a shrine for humanity.

I wanted so desperately to do what I could for my mother. I made sure she always had enough to eat, paying a local diner for her meals. I gave her money. I accepted her collect calls. I drove into the city to take her for lunch, even though it terrified me to leave Nicole alone with a babysitter. We'd always meet at a nearby café or diner—I avoided the Armory as much as I could; the building intimidated me. It was a vast Victorian redbrick building with crenellated towers and Gothic arches. To enter, you had to walk downstairs to a discreet darkened door, through an area stacked with garbage, and up a series of steep metal stairs.

Now that she was living at the shelter, her obsession with religion and astrology became even more pronounced. She spoke often about the planets, about their movements, how everything was predestined. She liked to talk about "the Father" and how important He was in her life. "The Father" was always telling her what to do, and she was determined to follow His instructions. Other times she would talk about "They." "They want me to do this," she'd say, or, "They said I should do that." When I asked her whom she was talking about, she wouldn't tell me.

"We'll talk about it when the sun is shining," she used to say.

She was constantly praying, constantly worried. Concerned that I was sick, that the children needed to go the doctor. I didn't tell my mother about what was happening with Nicole's health. I didn't want her advice or to have her tell me that we needed a miracle.

After we finished eating, we'd say good-bye, and I'd get back in my car and drive to the suburbs to try to go on with my life.

MY FATHER NO LONGER considered my mother his problem. Since the divorce, they'd had very little contact. To my knowledge, he didn't ever go to visit her during her time at the Armory, and he didn't give her money. Malcolm Reybold, once the dashing man-about-town who had captured my mother's heart, was in his seventies now and living back on Long Island.

He had already suffered multiple heart attacks when, in January of 1988, he had his fatal stroke. Jyl, Patricia, my mother, and I went to the funeral. My father and I had never been close; I knew my sisters felt the same way. At his open casket I wept, as much for the bond we'd never shared as for the man himself.

AT THE SHELTER, my mother kept to herself; she didn't speak to the other women who lived there. I think she no longer wanted to be measured or judged by anyone's standards. My mother living at the Armory wasn't ideal for anyone, least of all her. But with the distance of time, I can see that the shelter gave her, if nothing else, a roof over her head and the anonymity she craved.

At the Armory, she had found, in her own way, a place to hide and some peace.

Then, one day, as she was sitting on the steps of her favorite park, on Fifty-eighth Street, dressed all in white, my mother looked up and saw a camera lens pointing in her direction. She heard the familiar sound of the shutter's click, click, click.

She had been captured.

Part Two

❖

AFTER

CHAPTER 17

In the supermarket parking lot, I finished reading the article about my mother with the photo of her sitting on the shelter steps. By the time I closed the magazine's pages; I was trembling. PRINCESS GRACE BRIDESMAID LIVING IN NY SHELTER FOR HOMELESS. My mother's story was there in black and white, for everyone to see. How could I explain to people that my family's situation was far more complicated than a headline and a magazine article could even begin to convey?

This wasn't the last time my mother's story appeared in print. In 1989, the same year as the magazine article, a book was published about Grace and her six bridesmaids. It was written by Judy Balaban Quine, one of the bridesmaids herself. *The Bridesmaids: Grace Kelly, Princess of Monaco, and Six Intimate Friends* followed each of their stories, including my mother's. While Judy was working on the book, she had called to ask for an interview with me. At the time, I had said no. Back then, I didn't feel that anything good could come from my mother's story being out in the world.

When the book was released, however, I bought it immediately and read it closely. Judy described my mother's upbringing in Steubenville, her time as a model, her marriage to my father. She was kind and gracious in her depiction of my mother's descent from bridesmaid to shelter, but even so, there was much she didn't know or wouldn't say about Carolyn's struggles.

For me, the book answered some questions and raised many others. In one section of the book, Judy mentioned that my mother had kept her daughters home from school due to illnesses. Memories of my years spent at home came flooding back to me. Was it possible I had missed as much time as I thought? How reliable was my memory of events?

I could no longer ask my father. If I asked my mother, I knew, her answers would only confuse me further. Jyl had been so much older than me; she had been busy with her own life by the time my absences became a real problem. As I tried to make sense of what was being written about my mother, I realized that I had no context for what had happened to me as a child. I had simply been too young to understand.

Perhaps if I applied for my school records, this might at least give me some concrete information. I called my high school, Cold Spring Harbor High. They confirmed they had my records. Not long after that, I drove out to Long Island. The woman in the office had the records waiting for me. I remember she commented that she'd never seen a folder as thick as mine; there were more than a hundred pages. She let me use the Xerox machine, and I carefully copied each record before driving home. Later that day, I took the pages to my room and began to read. Here were letters from the school principal begging my mother to send me to school. Letters from my mother canceling the tutors who were coming to my home to teach me. Letters from doctors confirming I was sick. Letters from doctors explaining that I was healthy. More than one hundred pages documenting the months and years of missed education, the failed attempts of the school to force my mother to send me to my classes.

I knew with certainty now that my mother had kept me home for the majority of my childhood without any real cause. Perhaps I had some minor legitimate health issues over the years, but nothing that warranted keeping me away from school for months on end.

After I'd finished reading the school records, I didn't see my mother again for a number of months. I was too upset. Each morning I looked at my own children getting ready to go to school, and I tried to understand how a young girl could be denied an education for so many years without anyone coming to her rescue. I was angry with my mother, but I was also furious with my father, my school, the child welfare system—in fact, with anyone who'd failed to intervene on my behalf. The cost had been my education, the basic right of every child.

But the more I learned about my mother's illness, the more I came to understand the role it had played. When she acted in such strange ways, had she been hearing voices in her head, telling her what to do? When she was anxious and withdrawn, was mental illness to blame? People with paranoid schizophrenia often hear voices; they can be anxious; they suffer from delusions. Did my mother imagine my illnesses? Were they just a part of her delusions?

I knew that in order to have any kind of relationship with her in the future I needed to talk to her about what I had learned. On Mother's Day 1990, I decided I was ready. I arranged to meet my mother at the square on Fifty-eighth Street where she went each day to sit and pray. Then we walked together to the nearby diner for lunch, sitting down in the back room.

My mother began her usual update, telling me about the movement of the planets. On any other day, I would have done my best to listen, while avoiding meeting her eyes. This time, I looked at her squarely.

"Mom, I've seen my school records," I said. "I know everything."

For the first time, I talked openly with my mother about what had happened to me as a child.

"I want you to know that there was nothing wrong with me all those years ago," I explained. "I was never sick. You kept me home for no reason."

My mother turned and looked at me.

"You were having delusions," I went on. "I know it wasn't your fault. It was your illness."

I explained to my mother that there were medications that could help her, if she would only take them.

"I want you to know that I forgive you," I told her. "I have a good life now."

I waited. I saw the recognition in her eyes, and I knew she had understood me.

Finally, my mother spoke. She had tears in her eyes.

"That's a lot for a person like me to handle," she said.

Did my mother understand what she had done by keeping me home all those years? I didn't push her any further. We had come far enough—I had said what I needed to say.

THAT SUMMER, my mother's mother—my grandmother, Dorothy—passed away from colon cancer. I gave my mother money for the airfare so she could say goodbye. I didn't go to the funeral; I couldn't leave the children.

My daughter, Nicole, was still struggling. Along with her seizures, she was experiencing serious developmental delays. We went to every doctor, tried every medication, every possible approach.

In 1995, when she was eleven years old, Nicole underwent brain surgery to remove an abnormal area of cells that her doctors thought might be causing the seizures. During the surgery, her surgeon discovered a tumor that had been there since birth. After the tumor was removed, the seizures stopped, but Nicole developed psychiatric problems. She was frequently disturbed; she began hearing voices; we were dealing with behavioral issues. She was diagnosed with symptoms of schizophrenia. Nicole started at a day-treatment program for severely emotionally disturbed children; it was a caring, supportive place where the staff did everything they could for her. Thanks to the program, I began to go to see a therapist with Nicole each week. This was the first time in my life that I had access to mental health professionals, and I began to understand what it meant to advocate for someone's care.

I was the mother of three now—my younger daughter, Danielle Robyn, named for my sister, had been born in 1991. Since having my children, I had thrown myself into my role as mother, determined to be involved in their life in ways my own mother had never been. The same was true of my marriage. I had tried to be the perfect wife for my husband. I got up in the morning, I dressed the part, I said the right words, and I smiled at the right times. But now, at the age of thirty-six, I realized that, at my core, I was deeply unhappy.

I decided to start having sessions with a therapist for myself. The therapist asked me, "Nyna, when you look in the mirror, who do you see?" I sat for quite some time trying to get the words out before I realized there was no way for me to answer that question.

The therapist explained to me that in order to begin to find the answer, I was going to have to look back. She helped me to see that, like so many women, I was terrified of becoming my mother. That despite all my efforts to escape my mother's influence, I had inadvertently followed in her footsteps. I had left home at a young age, just as my mother had done. I had modeled, just as she had done. I had given up my career to move out of the city and focus on being a wife and a mother, just as she had given up her career. I had three children, just like my mother. If she could crack—slipping through the fragile net of life—what was stopping me from doing the same?

I knew what came next in the story, and I was determined to do everything in my power to avoid it. My children were depending on me.

FOR MORE THAN a decade, my mother lived at the shelter by choice. No one could legally force her to leave, as much as we tried. But then, in the summer of 1998, that choice was taken away from her. She collapsed in the street and was taken to Lenox Hill Hospital, where the doctors discovered that she had heart problems and needed a pacemaker. She refused to let them fit her with one, and no one could persuade her to change her mind. At this point, the shelter staff explained that without the pacemaker, they could no longer take care of her, and for legal reasons she wouldn't be allowed to come back to the shelter. By now, my experiences with Nicole had taught me how to be an advocate. I worked closely with my mother's social worker to find a place for her, locating an adult home in Sachem on Long Island where she could be cared for. I knew my mother was going to miss Manhattan and her routine there, but I also knew that for the first time in many years she was going to be someplace safe.

My mother traveled to the adult home in an ambulance, so she would have medical supervision while in transit. I drove ahead, so I could be waiting for her when she arrived. I remember staying to help her set up her room, like a parent with a child going away to college. It didn't take us long to get her settled; she had hardly any possessions, just a few items of clothing, her watercolor set, and some books. I made sure she was comfortable and had been introduced to all the staff. Then we said our good-byes. I hugged my mother and told her I would come back soon, holding her in my arms. She was so tiny, so fragile.

For so many years, I had wanted my mother to be a mother to me. I longed for her to do all the things I saw other mothers doing for their adult children. Even a simple interaction, such as going for lunch and catching up, was so fraught and complicated for my mother and me. When she couldn't provide these most basic aspects of motherhood, I had felt so sad and frustrated. But that day at the adult home, I understood. I could no longer expect her to play the role of mother in my life. *I* needed to be the parent now.

In the months to come, I drove out to see her as much as I could. She would often ask me to bring her items she needed, something to wear, a new pair of shoes, a book. Once I brought her a cassette player as a gift, along with some of the classical ballet tapes that I knew she loved. The next time I visited, I noticed the cassette player and the tapes were still in their packages. Didn't she want to listen to the music? My mother shook her head. I think she felt that she didn't deserve such pleasures anymore.

Adjusting to life in an adult home wasn't easy for my mother, but there were benefits for her. One of them was that she finally began taking medication. The nurses would sit with her and make sure she took every single one of her pills—and she became much more stable as a result. For the first time since her diagnosis, she was actually being treated.

The move to the adult home marked a turning point in my life, too. I was determined to finally look in the mirror and to find myself there. I began establishing myself professionally, creating a new career for myself in advertising sales, working for a local newspaper for a boss who became a real mentor to me. For the first time I began to acknowledge that I wasn't happy with myself *or* in my marriage. A year after my mother moved to the adult home, David and I filed for divorce. I put my focus on my children and becoming fully independent. My lack of education haunted me, but I could no longer let it stand in my way. I knew I had choices that my mother never had—to work and provide for my children and myself now that my marriage had run its course.

Five years later, when I met the man who would become the love of my life, I didn't try to hide my past from him. I didn't want to fit anyone's idea of "perfect" anymore. Like me, Peter had three children and was divorced. He understood.

Early in our relationship, I let Peter know that I came with a lot of baggage.

"Bring it on," he told me. "One bag at a time."

NOT LONG AFTER I met Peter, my mother was diagnosed with colon cancer like her mother before her. She was moved to a nursing care center in Medford, New York, where she would be able to receive around-the-clock care. By then, she was so frail she could barely walk; the nurses would put her in a wheelchair to take her into the dining room. They were so kind to her at Medford; they took good care of her and made the last years of her life as comfortable as possible.

It was during the time my mother was living at Medford that I got a phone call from a writer working on a biography of Grace Kelly. The writer wanted to interview my mother about her friendship with Grace. Up to this point, I had always refused to talk to writers and reporters; in the years since my mother's story had first appeared in the press, there had been articles in the *New York Post* and *Hello* magazine. TV shows such as *Hard Copy* and *Current Affair*

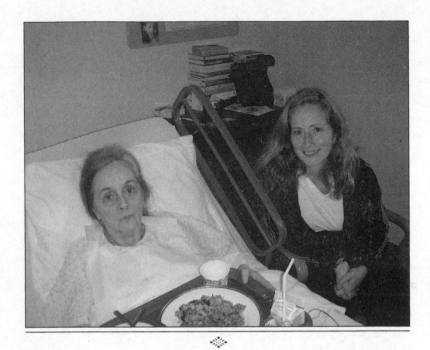

had run segments on her situation. And in all this time, I hadn't spoken to a single reporter. I'd always wanted to protect my mother from their questions, from the prying eyes of the world. But this time, I felt differently. My mother was no longer living at the shelter; she was on medication now, and although she was struggling physically, she was much more stable mentally. I thought she might enjoy sharing memories of Grace. Why not? I called my mother at the nursing care center and asked if she would be interested in being interviewed. She said yes—and so a few weeks later, I arranged to go with the writer for the visit.

That afternoon, I sat and listened as the writer asked my mother questions and my mother answered them. My mother, who usually didn't like to talk about the past, told the writer story after story.

She remembered the first time she saw Grace coming out of the re-volving doors at the Barbizon Hotel, the color of her coat, the sprig of blue flowers in her hat. She told the story of how she encouraged Grace to go into modeling so Grace could have some financial inde-pendence from her father. She could recall the night she had seen Grace in her Broadway debut, how she had sat in the front row of the theater with Malcolm.

"When she walked out onto the stage, looking so fresh and pretty," my mother remembered, "I burst into tears. I think it was then I realized she was going places."

My mother smiled, recalling the time she suggested Grace wear her hair swept back from her face in a chignon, a style that became her signature.

As the afternoon drew on, I knew I should probably ask the writer to leave; I could see my mother was growing tired. But I was enjoy-ing listening to the stories. I didn't want this to end.

Then the conversation took a different turn. The writer had been saving one question for last.

"I heard somewhere that there was an affair between Malcolm and Grace," she pressed. "Is it true?"

I should have stopped the conversation right there. I should have told my mother not to answer the question. Instead I froze.

"Yes," my mother replied, tears welling in her eyes. "It's true."

As my mother spoke, the writer scribbled down every word in her notebook.

"Grace asked me to come to the Manhattan Hotel," my mother said. "She was visiting New York. She told me what had happened. She wanted me to forgive her. 'You don't have to worry,' Grace told me. 'We're no longer an item!' I left the hotel in tears and ran straight to my therapist's office."

I reached for my mother's hand.

"It wasn't Grace's fault," my mother insisted, turning to me. "Your father was a tricky man."

At this point, I asked the writer to stop the tape machine. I knew the conversation had already gone too far.

The biography came out the following year. In the book, the writer focused on the alleged affair, overlooking all the other elements of the friendship that had been so important to my mother. After the book was released, I glanced at the sections about my mother and then put it away. Even the thought of what she had written about the affair was too confusing, too painful.

AT THE NURSING HOME, my mother's health took a rapid turn for the worse. She weakened very quickly. I remember going to see her at the hospital where she had been taken for tests. Jyl had been called there, too. Our mother was conscious but barely able to speak, propped on pillows in her bed. We spoke with her doctors, trying to figure out how to make her comfortable, what to do next.

That day, I remember, my sister had brought along a framed photograph of our mother in her modeling days. The photo had been given to Jyl by relatives. I had never seen anything like it before. In the photo, my mother was still in her twenties, wearing a pale blue dress embroidered with white flowers and holding a matching lace parasol, her dark eyes looking slightly upward. The picture was from the cover of *McCall's* magazine dated August 1948. After I got home from the hospital that day, I found the same issue of *McCall's* on eBay, bid on it, and won. When the magazine arrived, I had it framed and hung it on my dressing room wall.

Not long after that, we learned she needed a feeding tube in order to eat, but she was refusing to let the doctors insert it. In the coming days, she drifted in and out of consciousness. I remember the final phone call, the nurse telling me to come to the nursing care center right away; they didn't know how much longer my mother had left. I drove there immediately. I remember walking into the room and seeing my mother in her bed, so tiny under the expanse of covers, her mouth opening and closing like a bird. I sat with her. I held her hand. I told her I loved her, that I didn't want her to go.

My mother died that night. She was seventy-nine.

We didn't have a funeral for her. My father and Robin were gone. There weren't any friends or family left to invite that we knew of. Jyl and I decided to split her ashes. I remember going to the funeral home, where they gave me a gold box filled with my half, along with a poem titled "In Loving Memory of Carolyn Reybold, the Rose Beyond the Wall."

> *Near a shady wall a rose once grew,*
> *Budded and blossomed in God's free light,*
> *Watered and fed by the morning dew,*
> *Shedding its sweetness day and night.*

I knew it was most likely the same poem they printed out for all the families, but the words moved me all the same. The rose beyond the wall, my beautiful mother, always out of my reach.

CHAPTER 18

After my mother's death I went through a period where I couldn't be alone without breaking down. If I got in my car and my husband or children weren't with me, I would start to cry and couldn't stop, the sobs taking over my entire body until I couldn't even turn the ignition, let alone get out of the driveway. I met with a psychologist who didn't believe in medication, and he told me I needed to think positive thoughts whenever I felt the sadness coming on. This didn't work. Eventually, my internist prescribed a course of medication, and that helped me to feel stronger. But no matter what I did, I couldn't change that my mother was gone and that the losses of the past had outlived her.

When someone so close to you dies, you reach for whatever you can find of that person, just to keep them with you a bit longer. But there was so little I had left of my mother. By the time she died, she had very few possessions remaining, just a handful of photographs of my children I had given her, some books, and some items of clothing. There were no remnants of her youth, no jewelry, no letters; even the bridesmaid's dress had gone. And besides the framed cover of the magazine on my wall, there weren't any other pictures from her modeling days.

I began to spend my weekends at the New York Public Library, going through old copies of *Seventeen* and *Mademoiselle* searching for her image. The librarian would bring me bound volumes of magazines, and then I would turn the pages, looking for her and finding her over and over again. Each time I saw her face, I recognized her immediately, the beautiful young woman in the photograph, turning to look at the camera. But what had happened to that smiling, hopeful girl? Where had she gone? I had never known her.

My children were getting older. After Nicole turned twenty-one, she moved into a group home with five other housemates with developmental disabilities. My son moved across the country, to L.A., to pursue a career as an actor. Danielle went away to college to study fashion merchandising.

I had time now, time to see what else I could find of my mother, to look for her traces.

THERE WAS A thin mask of snow on the banks of the Ohio River and a weak sun pushing through ice-gray clouds as I drove across the bridge to Steubenville that day. I was returning to my mother's hometown for the first time since she'd brought me here as a young child. Back then, we had been running away from my father, from the school officials hounding her with telephone calls and letters.

This time, I'd arranged to meet the president of Steubenville's historical society, Charlie Green, at the small library and museum that he helped to manage. When I'd asked over the phone if he had any materials relating to my mother, Charlie laughed. Didn't I know? There was a permanent display devoted to my mother at the society, as well a number of files in the archives. A few years back— not long after my mother's death—the historical society had even hosted an evening honoring Carolyn and her legacy. They had displayed photographs of my mother, and friends who remembered her had given toasts. No one knew how to contact me, or they would have invited me to come.

I said I wished more than anything I could have been there.

The day of my visit, I parked outside the historical society, housed in an old redbrick mansion on Steubenville's Franklin Avenue. Charlie was waiting for me there. He was a tall and gracious silver-haired gentleman; the library and museum was generally closed around this time of year, but he was opening it especially for my visit, and I thanked him for the kindness. Charlie took me through the oak-paneled entry room directly to the room where my mother's photograph was kept on a low walnut-wood piano, in a heavy silvered frame. The picture was from 1947, the year that Carolyn was crowned Queen of Steubenville. In the photo, my eighteen-year-old mother is wearing a black-and-white-striped skirt and a cropped black top, her hair sleek and full. It's summer, and she's standing side-long to the camera, with hands behind her back, looking out at the world with such a simple and straightforward happiness. She's about to leave for New York, ready for the adventure ahead of her.

Although Charlie hadn't known my mother personally, he knew about her story.

"Everyone my age who grew up in Steubenville knows about Carolyn," Charlie told me. "She was our Sesquicentennial Queen!"

Then Charlie led me to a back room, crammed with filing cabinets and boxes, where he pulled out an album devoted to Steubenville's 150th anniversary celebrations. We looked through the pages together, finding photograph after photograph of my mother, sitting on her silvered throne, wearing a long embroidered velvet cape, a crown on her head, and carrying a large bouquet of long-stemmed roses as proudly as any scepter. Charlie had even unearthed my mother's high school yearbook, her photo still unfaded, preserved with all the freshness of youth. Then he handed me a large file marked CAROLYN SCHAFFNER; inside were clippings from magazines, advertisements from her modeling days, features from *Seventeen* and *Charm*. There was the cover of *McCall's* taken by Avedon, the Coca-Cola advertisement that my father had helped to arrange. I went through the pictures one by one, some of them new to me, each one a treasure.

Then, at the back of the folder, was a clutch of articles from the late 1980s and early 1990s, the period when my mother was staying at the shelter. I had guessed they would be there. FROM FAIRY-TALE TO FLOPHOUSE, the headlines read.

Charlie looked at me with kind eyes. A true gentleman, he didn't press me for more information.

But there was one last item he wanted to show me. We went to his small office at the back of the building to sit down. Here he pulled out two letters. I think it had taken him a while to work up the courage to show them to me.

The first letter was from Congressman Doug Applegate, writing to the mayor of Steubenville, Bill Croskey, about my mother in 1989. It turned out that both Doug and Bill had been in high school with my mother. After the news broke that Carolyn Schaffner was living in a shelter, they decided to rescue her. Doug had written to the mayor of New York, Ed Koch, asking for his help bringing Carolyn back to Steubenville. Mayor Koch had responded. He wrote that had looked into the matter but had learned that Carolyn had resisted all efforts to provide her with housing and that nothing further could be done. Doug and Bill were forced to drop their attempt to bring Steubenville's queen back home.

I had no idea that the town's representatives had written to the mayor of New York to ask for his help. That they had tried to do this for her touched me more than I could explain to Charlie. She had been appreciated by her hometown in ways I had never imagined.

After I finished reading the letters, I told Charlie about my mother's illness and the role it had played in her life. I felt that by telling him, I had brought him information that he hadn't been able to locate in all his files and archives. He nodded; a true historian, he understood. I thanked him for his generous hospitality—and for the tributes to my mother that meant so much to me.

After I left the historical society, I drove the short distance to Pennsylvania Avenue, to the street where my mother had grown up. The row houses were exactly as I remembered them, each one identical to the next, with steep banks leading up to front porches and peaked gables. I pulled up outside 1416 Pennsylvania Avenue, where I'd visited my grandmother with my mother as a small child. I stepped out of the car. The air was frozen, the ground hard underfoot. My grandmother was long gone. I stood outside, looking up at the building, wishing for some kind of sign. But nothing stirred, not a twig on a tree, not even a bird in flight. Turning around, I saw a small corner store with its windows boarded up across the street. I realized this was the old candy store where my mother had taken me when I was a child.

That weekend, I was able to reconnect with family members I hadn't seen in many years. I met with my mother's cousins Patricia and Jacqueline, who had been close to her during her childhood and teens. They remembered my mother with nothing but affection and love. They told me about Carolyn's stepfather and his curfews: when she came home too late Joe locked the door, and she would have to walk three miles to their house to stay the night. I spent time with the daughter of my mother's half brother, my cousin Tracy. She remembered going with my uncle to New York to look for my mother when she had been living in the shelter, trying to track her down, to bring her home. Her entire family had been so worried about her. No one had known what to do.

AFTER I RETURNED to New York, I went on with my research. I spent hours searching for my mother's image in magazines. I traveled to the Library of Congress in Washington, D.C., to the libraries at the Fashion Institute of Technology and the Metropolitan Museum of Art in New York, going through dozens and dozens of back issues. I learned that during the years of her career—1948 to 1956—Carolyn Scott appeared in hundreds of advertisements, and catalogs. I connected with a fashion historian who told me that Richard Avedon had taken the photograph of my mother from the cover of *McCall's*—the one that I kept on my dressing room wall. The historian confirmed that my mother was one of the first Ford models and that her success had helped Eileen Ford to build her agency.

I made contact with Eileen herself, then in the last months of her life. I knew that she must remember my mother because Eileen had been interviewed for the *Hard Copy* segment about my mother's story back in the 1990s. In the interview, Eileen described my mother as "one of the most successful junior models we ever had . . . a sort of a golden girl, living that wonderful life." When the interviewer asked why she thought Carolyn was living at the shelter now, Eileen said she believed Robin's death had a lot to do with it. "She was just destroyed," Eileen explained. "And it's hard for me to sit here and talk to you and not cry, because it really is a tragedy."

After I reached out to Eileen, she invited me to visit her at her apartment on the Upper East Side. Although she was in her nineties by then, frail, with her memory fading, she was still dressed immaculately in a white blouse, pale pink slacks, and a pink sweater. She remembered my parents in their Manhattan House days, how my father always knew exactly what to order at restaurants, and how they went out dancing, all of them together, sometimes until four in the morning. She could recall coming out to our house on Long Island many times in the early years. And she remembered seeing my mother around the neighborhood when Carolyn was living at the Park Avenue Armory shelter. Sometimes Carolyn would recognize Eileen; other times not.

"She used to go to the ladies' lounge at Bergdorf's to wash," Eileen told me.

A pained look came across Eileen's face at the memory. Later, as I got up to leave, Eileen took my hand.

"You're Carolyn's little girl," she said. "She would have been so proud."

As I thanked Eileen, I had tears in my eyes. This compliment from her, someone I admired so much and who knew my mother in her modeling days, meant more to me than I could say.

That day, I left Eileen's apartment and walked the few short blocks south to East Sixty-third Street and the Barbizon Hotel. The hotel itself closed its doors in 1981, its modest single rooms now converted into luxury apartments. At the lobby and mezzanine levels— where my mother had once taken afternoon tea with the other residents—there was now an Equinox gym. Gone were the gilded revolving doors where Carolyn first spotted Grace all those years ago, replaced by flat glass panels instead. Of course Mrs. Sibley, the hotel manager, and Oscar, the doorman, were gone, too, the lobby area reduced to a small entryway with elevators. I had read somewhere that a handful of former Barbizon residents still lived in the building, grandfathered in when the hotel had been converted into condos. I asked the doorman if I could leave my name and number with him on the very slim chance that someone remembered my mother. The following week, I received a call from a woman who had lived in the building since 1965—for more than fifty years—but not long enough to remember Carolyn.

Before I left the Upper East Side that day, I knew there was one more place I needed to visit. I walked back uptown, passing the diner on Lexington Avenue where I used to meet with my mother for our lunches, until the Armory's tall redbrick towers came into view. I stood on the corner of Sixty-sixth Street and Lexington; the Barbizon was just a few blocks south, the Manhattan House to the east. Until this moment, it had never occurred to me that these significant landmarks in my mother's life—the Manhattan House, the Barbizon Hotel, and the shelter—were all within five minutes' walk of one another. Their locations were fixed points in the constellation of my mother's greater journey. No wonder she wanted to live at the Armory all those years, and no one could persuade her to move. These few blocks of the Upper East Side were the place where she had made her mark and where she had been happiest. To her, this was home.

I KEPT SEARCHING for new insights, more information, but as hard as I tried to put the parts of my mother's life back together, there were some pieces that still wouldn't fit. I knew that in order to fully understand her story, I needed to figure out the point at which my mother first began to show symptoms of her illness. From my reading about paranoid schizophrenia, I knew that in the vast majority of cases, symptoms of the disease begin to show in late adolescence or one's early twenties. But when I met with my mother's friends and family members, I always asked if they noticed any signs of strange behavior on my mother's part when she was younger, in her teens and twenties—and they always told me no. From what I knew of my mother, she only began showing signs of her illness *after* I was born. By then, she was thirty years old. Was it typical for someone with schizophrenia to have such a late onset? Could the illness have been triggered in some way by my birth and the hysterectomy she'd had at the same time? A friend who worked in the mental health field offered to introduce me to someone at Columbia University Medical Center, who in turn connected me with one of the foremost experts on schizophrenia, Dr. Jeffrey Lieberman, chairman of the Department of Psychiatry at Columbia. I hoped that if I gave him detailed information about my mother, Dr. Lieberman would be able to help answer my questions.

On the day of our appointment, Dr. Lieberman welcomed me into his office, lined with shelves of books and with windows overlooking the waters of the Hudson River. I sat down on the couch and began to tell Dr. Lieberman as much as I could about my mother, about her childhood in Steubenville, her move to New York. I explained there had been no signs of her illness until after my birth. I brought with me the names of the medications I knew she had taken for her illness after she had moved to the adult home. I explained that she had only been diagnosed as mentally ill much later in life and that throughout my childhood and early adulthood, we had no idea what was wrong with her.

"In order to diagnose mental illness, there isn't an ironclad test," Dr. Lieberman told me. "You can't take a blood test or perform an MRI to determine the nature of someone's disease. Instead, you have to rely on symptomatic evidence."

He asked me many questions. Did my mother suffer with insomnia? Did she smoke? Did she have a history of hypochondria? Did she experience any trauma in childhood? Did she have any religious beliefs?

I answered his questions. I explained that by the time my mother received her diagnosis of paranoid schizophrenia, she was in her fifties. She had been taken to the hospital because she seemed to be having some kind of psychotic episode.

"The doctors there would have seen a woman who was delusional, and so they made their diagnosis based on the symptoms she was presenting to them," Dr. Lieberman said. "But presumably they wouldn't have had access to her prior history and health records?"

I told him no.

Dr. Lieberman paused, then spoke.

"You mother didn't have paranoid schizophrenia," he said. "What you've just described to me are the symptoms of postpartum psychosis."

I was stunned. I had always been told that my mother was schizophrenic, and yet here I was in the presence of the world's foremost authority on the disease, and he was suggesting a completely different diagnosis.

Dr. Lieberman went on to describe postpartum psychosis, a severe psychiatric condition that can set in during the first month after a mother gives birth to a child, even more serious than the more common postpartum depression.

"Women with postpartum psychosis can experience depression, but also mania, confusion, paranoia, hallucinations, and delusions," Dr. Lieberman explained. "Some women actually go on to cause physical harm to the infant—even killing the child—but the delusions can take many forms."

I explained that my mother had never done anything to deliberately harm me; her delusions were only related to my physical health. Dr. Lieberman explained that my mother may have had tendencies toward hypochondriasis and other types of obsessive-compulsive behavior even before my birth, but that the postpartum psychosis would have exacerbated those tendencies, magnifying their effect.

"Today, we consider postpartum psychosis temporary and treatable," Dr. Lieberman told me. "If left untreated, however, the sufferer only continues to deteriorate, as your mother did."

At the end of our session, I thanked Dr. Lieberman for his time and insights, then left his offices.

I had spent so many years looking for reasons, trying to figure out why my mother had behaved the way she did, why she was so closed off and disconnected, why she'd kept me home all those years.

Now I knew.

The reason had been me.

CHAPTER 19

That day after leaving Dr. Lieberman's office, I climbed into my car and pulled away into traffic, but it was hard to focus on the road through tears. As soon as I could, I pulled off and parked the car again. I walked into a store, trying to collect myself enough to continue the drive home. It was a while before I got back in the car.

When I finally arrived at my house, I went to my computer and looked up the symptoms for postpartum psychosis:

> *Delusions or strange beliefs*
> *Hallucinations (seeing or hearing things that aren't there)*
> *Feeling irritated*
> *Decreased need for or inability to sleep*
> *Paranoia and suspiciousness*
> *Rapid mood swings*
> *Difficulty communicating*
> *Obsessive concern over the infant*

It was as if someone who had met my mother was describing her to me.

In the coming weeks, I spoke with one of the leading experts on postpartum psychosis, Dr. Diana Barnes. I told Dr. Barnes my mother's story, and she confirmed Dr. Lieberman's diagnosis. We spoke at length about my mother's symptoms and about the impact of the surgery she underwent at my birth.

"As a model, your mother's whole persona was about femininity and beauty, so the hysterectomy would have been particularly hard for her," Dr. Barnes pointed out. "She would have felt she had lost part of what made her a woman."

Dr. Barnes explained to me that during the years when my mother first became sick, postpartum psychosis simply wasn't understood the way it is now; it would have been extremely difficult for anyone to treat my mother with any degree of accuracy. The tragedy of my mother's story is that the prognosis for her postpartum psychosis would have been much better than for paranoid schizophrenia; if she could have been treated, it's likely that she would have recovered.

I decided to visit my trusted ob-gyn, Dr. Dominic Grecco, someone I had been seeing for more than a decade, to learn more about the double surgery my mother had undergone at my birth. We talked through the C-section and the hysterectomy in detail.

"After such a traumatic surgery," Dr. Grecco explained, "it is highly unlikely that your mother could have escaped some kind of postpartum depression."

The doctor told me that because I was such a big baby, the massive incision would have limited her ability to breastfeed and bond with me. It would have been many weeks before the incision healed and she felt better in any way.

"Your birth was the fork in the road," Dr. Grecco went on, "the turning point in her life from which she never recovered."

THE NEW DIAGNOSIS brought me a greater understanding, but also another kind of loss—the knowledge of what might have been. I began to imagine another version of my mother's life where she could have been helped. In all likelihood, she would still have suffered with some kind of depression. Her life was filled with so many challenges: a cruel stepfather; a career that ended abruptly; a difficult, lonely marriage; the sudden deaths of Robin and Grace. But even so, I have to believe that in this alternate version of events, she might have prevailed.

I began to wonder how it must have been for my father to be married to someone who changed so completely after my birth. I decided to reach out to one of his friends from the time we were living on Long Island. Ross Meurer was an artist; he had been quite a bit younger than my father, and he was still living out in Cold Spring Harbor. We spoke over the phone. Ross told me how lonely and confused my father had been during the years my parents were still married. "Malcolm said he never knew which woman he was coming home to," Ross explained. "I think he missed the woman she'd been."

I'd always thought of myself as hidden away at home during my childhood, but as I spoke to Ross, I began to understand that my mother had been hidden, too. When she no longer fit with my father's vision of a happy, sociable, smiling wife, he simply stopped including her in his world. My father knew nothing about mental illness, let alone postpartum psychosis. He was a man of his times, completely lacking in any sensitivity or insight. I remember my father once pointing out to my sisters and me that if he'd had our mother committed to an asylum, we would never have forgiven him. This much was accurate. In some way, his complete neglect of our mother may have saved her from an asylum, and the inevitable shock treatments and prolonged hospitalizations that might have followed.

But there was one aspect for which I couldn't forgive my father. My poor mother had known something was wrong with her. She had started sessions with a psychiatrist in Manhattan immediately after my birth. When my father found the check stubs for the therapy, he'd said she couldn't continue, unless she went to a psychiatrist of his choosing. When she refused, he simply stopped the sessions altogether.

She had tried to get help, and my father had stood in her way.

I KEPT GOING back to the biographies of Grace. The more I read, the more questions I had. While Grace was solid and certain, with facts and figures, dates and details, Carolyn appeared for a paragraph or two, then vanished again. I dog-eared the pages with my mother's name so I wouldn't lose her. I was teasing out the fragments of her story from between the lines of Grace's; the fragile remnants of my mother's life were still slipping away and escaping from me.

More than one of Grace's biographers had written about the alleged affair between Grace and Malcolm. If those accounts were correct, then my mother first learned about the affair in the summer of 1960, just nine months after my birth. This was when she was still recovering from her C-section and hysterectomy, at the same time that she was experiencing her first symptoms of postpartum psychosis. I could only imagine how the news must have affected her at this time when she was already so fragile. And yet there was so much I didn't understand about what had taken place. When exactly had the affair happened? How long had it lasted? Had it even happened at all?

I could dimly remember visiting my sister Robin in Philadelphia once with my mother and hearing something about some kind of affair. I was about fourteen years old. Robin and my mother were in my sister's kitchen, sitting close together, talking intimately with each other as they often did. Grace's name was mentioned. I came closer, hoping to eavesdrop on their conversation. Then I *thought* I heard my mother say that Grace and my father had had an affair. But even then, it didn't make sense. My father and Grace? I couldn't reconcile the idea of Grace, the perfect princess in Monaco, with my father. When my mother and sister saw that I was listening, they quickly changed the subject.

All these years later, as I tried to learn the truth about what had happened, I discovered that there was very little evidence to go on. The only documentation I could find from that era was a Cholly Knickerbocker gossip column from January 1961, which claimed that all was not well between my parents that year:

"Malcolm Reybold, who at one time was a big name in Grace Kelly's life (in fact, Princess Grace confessed to his wife that they had been a romance), has now moved his quarters to the elegant Colony Hotel in Palm Beach. The reason—to establish residence for a divorce from his pretty brunette wife Carolyn, who was one of Grace's closest friends."

I was fourteen months old at the time. I have no recollection of these events, but if my father did move out, he must have come back again, as my parents stayed together for another thirteen years. In the book *The Bridesmaids,* Judy Balaban Quine writes that Grace insisted Malcolm invented the affair. "Grace had met Malcolm before he and Carolyn knew one another, but she had never gone out with him. She couldn't imagine why Malcolm would prolong this fiction of a romance between them, especially at a time when it might so wound Carolyn."

Another one of Grace's biographers seemed to suggest that the affair *did* take place but *after* Grace was married and living in Monaco. That just didn't seem feasible to me—how could Grace and Malcolm have managed it, living so many thousands of miles apart? Surely if something had happened between them it would have been when they were both living at the Manhattan House, years before Grace moved to Monaco. Was it possible my father had exaggerated details of the relationship and his connection to Grace in order to impress others? Was it possible that my mother was having delusions after my birth and invented the whole thing? I had seen the pain in my mother's eyes in the nursing care center when she talked about the affair; as if the betrayal had happened only yesterday. *I* believed her when she said the affair had taken place, but what evidence did I have beyond my mother telling me so?

The only people who could confirm the affair were Grace and Malcolm, and they both were gone. What I *did* know was that my mother never held anything against her friend. If there *was* an affair, she forgave Grace completely. And although Grace never came back to visit us on Long Island, the princess continued to write to my mother, and my mother continued to write letters in return. Despite the separation of miles and the troubles of the past, Grace and Carolyn's connection, forged in youth and hope, continued.

I DECIDED TO contact Judy Balaban Quine, Grace's close friend who had written the book about the princess and her bridesmaids.

We talked first on the phone. I told Judy that I wished I had spoken to her when she was working on her book, but I had been too afraid, too protective of my mother and her story. Now I understood the importance of connecting with the people who had known my mother—and I hoped we could meet in person soon. Judy invited me to visit her in Beverly Hills next time I was in Los Angeles to see my son. We arranged to meet at an Italian restaurant near her home. That day, Judy was waiting for me when I arrived, still elegant in her eighties, warm and bright-eyed. That night, we talked and talked. She was so compassionate, so understanding. I learned that in the course of researching her book, Judy had met with my mother while she was living at the shelter, interviewing her multiple times. They sat together in Central Park, or once, when it was raining, retreated to the Barbizon Hotel, where Judy rented a room for the afternoon so they could stay warm and dry. When my mother asked Judy to buy her some small items—socks and underwear—Judy set up an account at Bloomingdale's so that my mother could purchase whatever she needed. I had no idea that Judy had done this for my mother and I was so grateful.

Then I asked Judy about Grace. Judy explained to me that Grace had guessed something was very wrong with my mother's mental state after the move to Long Island, but like so many people, had no idea what to do or how to help. She reminded me that the 1960s and 1970s were a time when the stigma around mental health kept everyone in silence, not only sufferers but friends and relatives, too. Could Grace have done more for my mother? From a distance of thousands of miles, sequestered in her palace and her role as princess, what would have been possible? It was very hard to say.

That night, leaving the restaurant with Judy, I told her I wished we lived closer to each other. Being able to talk to someone who had known my mother *and* Grace, someone who cared about my mother, someone I could be completely open with, brought me a kind of comfort I had never experienced before.

DURING THIS TIME of searching and trying to understand the past, I found myself confronting questions that had dogged me for a lifetime. Growing up, I had been kept out of school for the majority of my childhood, by a mother with a severe mental illness. Why hadn't someone—the school, my father, the authorities—stepped in to save me? Why had it been up to *me* to remove myself from my mother's care?

I began to wonder how my case would have been handled if I were a child in the education system today. Would things have been different? Would the authorities have taken greater action? I arranged to go back to my old elementary school to meet with the principal there, to see if I could learn more. I knew that I couldn't fix the past by speaking with the principal—she hadn't even been working at the school when I was a child; I just knew it was something I felt strongly compelled to do.

The night before going back to the school, I had a dream. I was in the living room at my home. My husband asked me to pick up a blanket that had fallen to the floor. I tried to lift the blanket, but it was out of reach. I wanted to let Peter know that I couldn't pick up the blanket, but when I tried to speak, the words wouldn't come out. It was as if something was pressing down on me, suffocating me. The next time I reached for the blanket, I found myself being dragged in the opposite direction, as if I were going to slide away under the bookshelf and disappear. I tried to call out, but I couldn't make a sound. When I woke up, I was screaming, my head aching, my temples throbbing.

The following morning, I felt nauseous, anxious, bordering on panicky. I couldn't remember why I was putting myself through this! I didn't have a single positive memory from my time at elementary school. All I remembered was the feelings of sickening dread, being on the school bus and not wanting to go inside, afraid of not being accepted, of being bullied, of being embarrassed because I didn't know an answer in class. By the time I climbed into my car that afternoon to go to the appointment, I had to force myself to turn on the engine and make the drive south to Lloyd Harbor Elementary School.

When I arrived, it was just before the end of the day. I was a little early, so I sat in the parking lot for a while, watching as the mothers came to pick up their children. The students all looked so young, so innocent. I thought about how I often blamed myself for what had happened to me as a child, as if it had somehow been my fault that I had been kept home all those years. I remember deliberately telling my mother many times, "I don't want to go to school, I don't feel well," so she would keep me at home. But looking at the little children that day, I knew I couldn't blame myself anymore. They were so small, so completely dependent on the adults around them. How could a child be held responsible for his or her school attendance? That was a parent's job.

Eventually, I worked up the courage to go inside the building. Everything was so much smaller, much less intimidating than I remembered. I met with the assistant principal first. I asked him about how the school deals with attendance. He told me that if a child is as much as ten minutes late, the nurse is notified, and then a call automatically goes out to the parent. At the end of the week, the school office accounts for all absences. If the absences are longer than a few days, the school tries to meet with the family, and then a social worker and psychologist are called in before any legal action is taken. The assistant principal was matter-of-fact as he recounted the school's procedures to me—like an accountant reciting end-of-year numbers—but when I told him that as a child I had been absent from school as much as a full year at a time, he looked genuinely shocked and disturbed. Next, I met with the principal. I told her my story, too. She confirmed what the assistant principal had told me about the school's procedures. Then she paused.

"Are you angry about what happened to you as a child?" she asked.

I told her, yes. And I thanked her. In that moment, I felt a kind of validation and acknowledgment of what had taken place all those years ago. I was glad I'd come. Growing up, there had been so many invisible barriers and misunderstandings keeping my mother from seeking the help she needed. The visit to the school only strengthened my conviction that I had to channel my own experience into speaking out, to do whatever I could to break through silence, so that others wouldn't need to suffer as my mother and I had.

Climbing into my car, I felt as if something had shifted. I had gone back to a place that had terrified me so much as a child, only to find that there was nothing to be scared of anymore. I was a woman in my fifties now. I had three grown children. I was happily remarried with my husband's three children in my life as well. Driving home that day, I knew that despite the odds, I had made it.

CHAPTER 20

I kept going back, visiting all the places associated with my mother and my childhood, replacing each of the unhappy memories with new, more positive ones. By 2015, I had been to nearly everywhere on my list; Steubenville, Long Island, Philadelphia, and Manhattan included. But there was one last trip to make. I wanted to go to France, to the places I had visited with my mother and Robin when I was a young girl. And I wanted to go to Monaco, Grace's home for almost thirty years, to see the palace and the cathedral where the wedding took place, where my mother had stood beside her friend on the most important day of Grace's life.

When I visited France with my mother as a young girl, we never made it as far as Monaco. Monaco was a destination in a journey still unfinished.

In the years since my mother's death I had often thought about contacting Princess Grace's family, but I had never gotten up the courage to do so. Now I decided to write to Prince Albert—Grace's son—to tell him about my plans to visit. The prince's private secretary wrote back, explaining that while he would be out of the country during the dates of my stay, he had read my note. The secretary then said that she would like to arrange a private tour of the palace during my visit. I gratefully accepted. This acknowledgment of my mother and her friendship with Grace after so many years meant a huge amount to me.

In October 2016 I flew to Nice, traveling the short distance from the airport across the border to Monaco.

Until now, Monaco had always seemed as fantastical to me as an illustration from a fairy tale or one of the Technicolor scenes from Grace's movies. Now here I was, driving through the tiny streets of Monaco-Ville and Monte Carlo, the pink-and-yellow-painted buildings nestled into the hills surrounding a boat-filled harbor. It was late fall, and the colors were softer than I had expected in the gentle October sunlight. I visited the Hôtel de Paris, where my parents had stayed when they came for the wedding. I went for drinks at the hotel's American bar and ate in the Café de Paris across the square, where they gathered to socialize with friends.

On the morning of my palace tour, I stood outside Grace's former home under clouded skies, nervously waiting for the doors to open. The palace, painted a pale pink, was much smaller than I'd always imagined it to be. Ahead of me, smartly uniformed carabiniers guarded the way, and to my right, a crew of workers with jackhammers dug up the cobblestones outside the palace, the sounds of their drills echoing across the square.

At the entrance, a young woman in a navy-blue dress introduced herself. Her name was Marina, and she was my guide. We hurried through the security area so we could stay ahead of the school groups that would soon be following behind us. Marina led me through a small entranceway and up a narrow staircase to the palace's main gallery overlooking the courtyard. I recognized this place immediately: it was the Galerie d'Hercule, where Grace, my mother, and the other bridesmaids had posed for photographs immediately before the wedding ceremony. I had looked at those familiar black-and-white photographs so many times: the picture of Grace, standing at the marble balustrade, looking out over the palace courtyard, my mother in the background, keeping her within her sights. The group photographs with the little flower girls standing on either side of Grace, holding their bouquets in their little white gloves, my mother to Grace's far left. The photo where Grace stops to adjust my mother's hat, looking at her so tenderly.

Now I was standing in the same spot where those photographs had been taken, the grays of the past transformed into vivid life and color. What the black-and-white images had failed to convey was the jewel tones of the frescoes on every wall of the gallery, saturated with the deepest reds, yellows, and greens.

Following Marina, I walked through the rooms of the palace, each one filled with gilded French furniture, with chandeliers of cut Venetian glass hanging overhead. I stood in the throne room, with its red brocade walls and large golden throne, where Grace and Rainier's civil ceremony had taken place the day before their cathedral wedding. Above our heads there were murals depicting each of the signs of the zodiac, and in that moment, I was certain that both my mother and Grace would have approved of these astrological symbols, feeling reassured that the planets were watching over them that day.

In these hallways and rooms, Grace, the movie star and princess, finally became human to me. I imagined her here, walking as a wife and mother within her own home. To what degree had this palace been a gilded cage, as some of her biographers suggested? By all accounts, she was happy with her husband and her children—but she had sacrificed her career for her life here, and it was impossible to believe that there weren't days when she missed her work, her home in New York, her independent existence. Not long before her death, Grace confided to her friend Judy that she felt almost envious of my mother's freedom to come and go as she pleased while living in Philadelphia. These were the years when Carolyn struggled with stable housing, before she moved to the shelter.

"I know it might sound awful and insensitive," Grace explained. "But the thought of just getting up every day and doing what that day brings you sounds wonderful to me in certain ways."

Was it a mark of how tightly Grace's role as princess was circumscribed that she equated my mother's vulnerable situation with freedom and anonymity? I had read in Judy's book that it had been Grace's intention, just before her death, to find an apartment in Manhattan and live there for at least some part of each year. She missed New York, she told Judy. New York was *her* town, the city where she felt most herself. She even talked about starting her career again, maybe with a role on Broadway. Some part of her must have wished to recapture those formative years of youth, with their excitement and promise. Grace was due to come to New York in September 1982, to begin her search for an apartment, but she never made the trip. She died that same month, on September 14.

Three years later, when my mother arrived in New York to live at the shelter, she had been rounding a circle that even a princess had been kept from completing.

AFTER MONACO, I took the short train ride along the coast to Nice and Cannes, to see the places where I had stayed with my mother and Robin all those years ago. And from Cannes, I took another train, this time heading west, deeper into France. I was going back to Lourdes, to the place where my mother had taken my sister and me to find a cure.

At Lourdes, I visited Saint Bernadette's grotto, just as I had done with my mother and sister. Again I walked alongside the crowds of pilgrims, making their way to the shrine, with its white statue of the Virgin Mary that seemed to glow within the craggy rocks. I walked the narrow cobbled streets of the city, imagining my mother and how she must have felt when she came here, with two daughters and without money or plans for what would happen next. I tried to put myself in my mother's shoes: What did she think she was doing coming here? How did she think she would be able to make a life for herself in France? Everywhere I turned in Lourdes I was reminded of my mother: the statues of the saints; the people praying, their heads bowed and hands clasped; the gray and the white of the churches; the images of Saint Bernadette kneeling in prayer, submitting to a higher power. My mother believed in the saints, the Virgin, and the Holy Father, trusting in their absolute benevolence. I began to realize that from my mother's perspective, coming to Lourdes was the fulfillment of her dearest wish. She knew something was very wrong, and she truly believed that the shrine would give her the peace and healing she craved. Perhaps in her own way she understood more about her illness than I realized; perhaps she came to Lourdes, not only for a cure for Robin and me, but also for a cure of her own.

Later that afternoon, as I walked the streets of the city, I heard music coming from a nearby church. Curious, I walked toward the source of the singing, up the steps of the building and in through a tall, narrow archway. The church had high white stone arches and wide marble pillars. In the pulpit, a choir was singing, and in the pews, the congregants were singing, too. I didn't know the hymn but I heard the words "ave Maria," over and over.

I stood there, listening to the beauty of the music in the ancient church, the light streaming in through stained-glass windows like a blessing. In the past, I had always been a little skeptical about religion, at times even blaming my mother's faith for her obsession with prayer and miracles, fixations that I felt prevented her from confronting the reality of our situation. But standing in that church at Lourdes, I finally understood why her belief was so compelling to her. In that instant, I saw myself as she did, as a small dot in a much larger continuum of planets and time and cosmic influence, everything always moving, our fates not entirely in our own hands.

To my side there was an area with votive candles. I decided to light one for my mother and one for Robin. As the choir continued to sing, I bent to touch the taper to the wick, and the following words came into my head: "Stopped in to a church I passed along the way. . . . well, I got down on my knees and I pretend to pray. . . ." They were lyrics from one of Robin's favorite songs, "California Dreamin'." She used to sing it to me, strumming on her guitar. In that moment, I felt my sister was standing alongside me in the church, just as she had always done when she was alive, holding my hand, whispering in my ear.

I left the church and went back to my hotel. The next day, I was due to travel home to New York, but in so many ways, the journey was already over. I had gone to every place connected with my mother and her life. I had met her family, her friends, the people she had known as a model. I had met with medical professionals who had helped me to understand her illness. I had gone back to every memory of her from my childhood, and instead of turning away this time, I'd squared myself up to the past, asking every question, imagining every implication and scenario. It had been a long journey, and I was tired now, but there had been a reason for my persistence: I was trying to let my mother know how much I loved her, how much I still love her. I hoped she understood that. As I packed my bags and prepared to leave Lourdes, I knew with complete certainty that my mother loved me in return, that despite everything, she had been trying to do what she believed was best for me.

During this period of my research, I dreamt of my mother for the first time in years. In the dream, I was standing in the house on Long Island. I was alone. It was nighttime, and the room was very dark. I felt filled with fear, certain that something very bad was about to happen. I wanted to run away, but instead, I found myself drawn, as if by some invisible force, to the center of the house and then the kitchen. I looked up. I saw my mother, standing in a glow of pinkish-white light. She was beautiful, still young, dressed completely in white; she looked at me with so much love. I tried to say her name, but all I could get out was "Ma." When I woke up, I was still calling for her.

ACKNOWLEDGMENTS

My journey to write this book began on October 27, 2013, when I received a Facebook message from a stranger, Eve Claxton.

Eve told me that she was a writer, and she was hoping to write a book about the history of the Barbizon Hotel for Women. In the course of her preliminary research, Eve had stumbled on an article about Grace Kelly's stay at the hotel and her friendship with my mother. Since then, Eve had been attempting to track me down. It hadn't been easy for her to find me, as I had changed my name to Giles after marriage, but fortunately, Eve came across a photo of Grace's wedding on Flickr, with a comment left by my husband explaining that his wife was Carolyn's daughter. This had given Eve the clue to my married name.

Eve and I met for lunch shortly after. I told her that *I* had contemplated writing a book to honor my mother but could never summon the courage to do so, given the sheer complexity of the task. Not long after that, Eve and I decided to collaborate on a book, weaving together the years of Carolyn and Grace's friendship with my childhood memories and coming of age.

It was incredibly reassuring to me to see that Eve believed in my mother's story from the very beginning, which only served to build my own confidence, as we worked to put the pieces of the puzzle together. We interviewed anyone we could find who had known my mother. We spent countless hours digging into the archives of libraries and historical societies and trawled the deepest reaches of the internet. We were both equally passionate about *The Bridesmaid's Daughter* and about bringing the story to a wider audience.

Our deepening friendship made me realize over time that Eve is the only person who could have gone on this journey with me. I am so grateful to her for her patience, her perseverance, her amazing way with the written word, and her ability to always capture what was in my heart. I have had complete trust and faith in Eve, who ultimately made me feel safe in revealing this story. For all of these reasons, I will forever be in her debt.

So many others were involved in the creation of this book. I still can't believe that this very talented group at the top of their industry became my team, each helping to pull the stars into alignment for this book.

Emma Parry, our agent at Janklow & Nesbit. Emma, thank you for your calm guidance through the many, many drafts and versions— and for championing our story with such unwavering focus and dedication.

Hannah MacDonald, our editor at September Publishing. You saw the potential in my mother's story at a very early stage and gave us the opportunity to develop this book. Without your vision, the title you gave us, and your careful guidance throughout, we might never have found our way forward. Thank you for all your patience, hard work, and insight.

Charles Spicer, our editor at St. Martin's Press. Charlie, your belief in our project and your sensitivity and skill in bringing it to fruition have been a true gift to us. It was your conversation with Eve in 2012 that set her on the path of her Barbizon research, so it felt only right that the book should find its U.S. home with you at St. Martin's. Thank you for all the care you have taken with this project.

Thank you to our extraordinary publisher at St. Martin's, Sally Richardson, associate editor April Osborn, publicist Rebecca Lang, marketing manager Nancy Sheppard, marketing team leader Brant Janeway, William Rhino, assistant marketing manager, copy editor India Cooper, proofreader Kenneth Diamond, designer Kathryn Parise, production editor Elizabeth Catalano, and jacket designer Danielle Fiorella. At September, our thanks are also due to Charlotte Cole in editorial and Sue Amaradivakara in publicity.

Many thanks to our audio team: Mary Beth Roche, Laura Wilson, Robert Allen, Brisa Robinson, Samantha Edelson, and Margo Goody.

Kelly Shetron. Thank you for supporting this project from proposal stage through the early drafts when you sat for hours on the phone, helping us to pull together our research and stories.

Domenica Alioto. Thank you for your kindness, and for being a trusted sounding board at all stages of this book.

Writing *The Bridesmaid's Daughter* has been an amazing, challenging, and emotional journey that wouldn't have been possible without the invaluable guidance and loving support of so many others along the way. These wonderful people opened their hearts and welcomed me into their worlds, willingly giving of their time and sharing their intimate memories of my mother. Each successive interview served to reaffirm my own beliefs about my mother:

that she was a beautiful woman who should not be defined by her struggles, but rather by her success as a model and kindness as a person.

Judy Balaban Quine. Thank you for your book, *The Bridesmaids: Grace Kelly, Princess of Monaco, and Six Intimate Friends*. I often pick it up to read passages, and it has long been a bible to me, providing vital insight into my mother's past. Meeting with you and having subsequent conversations about this project has been enormously helpful. Knowing that you understood my reasons for wanting to tell this story, that we shared a passion for mental health advocacy, has brought me great personal strength. Many thanks also to bridesmaids Sally Richardson, Bettina Thompson, and the late Rita Gam.

I feel so lucky to have met and interviewed some of the most successful models of the 1940s and '50s while working on this book. My mother was one of the very first Ford models, so she joined an elite group of women who set the standard for beauty and poise during that era. Tippi Hedren shared her memories of working with my mother, and knowing how much fun they had together has brought me so much joy. In addition, Helen Ryan, Lorraine Davies, Millie Perkins, Bettie Johnson (and her husband, Don Murray), Lois Heyl Jewell, and Iris Bianchi Ory all provided valuable insights and perceptions of my mother and the industry.

Susan Link Camp and Patti Sicular. It would not have been possible to connect with my mother's peers without your help. Your work to honor the models of the 1940s and '50s is an inspiration to me. You included me at your model reunion luncheons, giving me the opportunity to meet women my mother had worked alongside and several of their daughters. I am deeply grateful for your help with my research, and for the many introductions to countless important resources, photographer's foundations, and archives. Susan, you graciously offered to share your vast collection of vintage fashion magazines with me so I could fill the gaps in my mother's career. For a period of six months, you shipped several vintage magazines at a time from California, which allowed me to take photographs before sending them back to you.

Another special experience was meeting model daughters Andrea Derujinsky (Ruth Neumann), Dinah Dillman Kaufman (Suzy Parker), Nelly Gimbel (Elinor Rowley), and Anna Murray (Patsy Shally). While I wasn't able to meet the fashion photographers my mother knew—as so many of them had already passed—I had the honor of connecting with two of their daughters: Pam Barkentin, daughter of George Barkentin, and Andrea Derujinsky, whose mother was a model and whose father was the photographer Gleb Derujinsky. Andrea, I am so grateful to call you my friend. It was shortly after we had met and bonded over lunch that I realized one of my favorite photos of my mother was taken by your father. I had gone to the New York Public Library to identify a few photos when I saw his name. I immediately texted you to let you know, and a tearful exchange ensued.

Eileen Ford. I am eternally grateful to Eileen for her role in my mother's success, and her help with my own career as a model. The afternoon I spent with Eileen toward the end of her life, when she shared memories of my mother, is one I will never forget.

Robert Lacey. Thank you for your kind support of this book. Your biography of Eileen Ford, *Model Woman*, is such a treasure to me. It's given me such insight into what my mother's life was like as a model. I was so moved and honored to see her remembered in the book as one of the top models of the 1940s and '50s.

Reconnecting with my mother's family has been such an important part of the journey. As a result, I feel as though I have truly met my family for the first time, and have made friends for life who have enriched me in so many ways. I am thankful to my cousin Tracy Hosfelt, my initial point of contact with the family, who reached out to me on Facebook in 2012. Tracy, thank you for sharing your photographs, memories, and insights, for meeting with us when we came to Steubenville, and for reconnecting me with my mother's cousin Sandra Hart.

Sandra Hart. It has been such a joy having you in my life. You've helped me understand who my mother really was, that she was truly a good person. A special gift along the way has been meeting your son, Emerson Hart, and your daughter, Brett Thompson. Emerson is the lead singer for the band Tonic—I had always loved Emerson's music, and it has been so wonderful to get to know him, to meet his family, and to go to his concerts. Your family truly understands the heartbreak mental illness brings, and having your support has meant a huge amount to me.

I am so grateful to my uncle, Terry Hosfelt, for sharing many photos and connecting me with my mother's cousins Patricia and Jacqueline.

Patricia James and Jacqueline Bendure. You shared so many wonderful memories of my mother as a young girl, and your love for her is so clear. I simply would have had no other way to have such incredible insight into her childhood and past. The time we spent together will forever be a treasured memory.

I'm thankful to have been in touch with Bill Kirkpatrick, Joyce Lee, and Donna Hosfelt. I'm also so grateful to have connected with Bobbi Baur, daughter of my mother's late half sister, Terri, and Bobbi's father, Jim Baur. Bobbi and Jim, thank you for sharing Terri's notes on my mother.

The City of Steubenville. Thank you for making my mother your

Sesquicentennial Queen all those years ago. It gave her a chance to pursue her dream of modeling. A warm thank-you to Charlie Green and Michael Giles for making our day at the Jefferson Historical Society in Steubenville so special. I'm so appreciative of the materials about my mother that you have preserved and shared with me, along with important contributions to the collection from Bill Croskey. Thank you to Rex Tate for being the driving force behind the 2008 tribute to my mother. Thank you to Dave Gossett from the *Steubenville Herald Star* who wrote an article explaining that I was looking for people who had known my mother, which helped me to connect with a number of her friends.

My mother's friends in Steubenville: Dottie Bossert, Jane McHugh Noltemeyer, Kay Gosseye, John Criss, and Nancy Peterson. Thank you for sharing your memories and your insights.

The organizers of the exhibit *From Philadelphia to Monaco: Grace Kelly Beyond the Icon* at the Michener Museum of Art. I feel so fortunate to have attended your "Last Look" event, where I was able to see photographs and artifacts from the royal wedding, and where I had a chance to meet Grace's nephew Chris Levine, who was so helpful prior to my trip to Monaco.

Profound thanks are due to Prince Albert of Monaco and the staff at the Prince's Palace of Monaco, including Christine Sprile, Christel Brizi, Yasmin Zagoni, and Marina Matkova. Thank you so much for our VIP private tour; we so enjoyed learning about the wonderful history of the palace. Thank you to Thomas Fuillerion and Olivia Oantoni at the palace archives for the materials you shared with us—it was a special pleasure to see the original seating plan for the cathedral wedding, including my father's name. Thanks also to Geraldine Byrne at the Princess Grace Irish Library in Monaco for her kind assistance.

Researching this book has given me a new appreciation and

renewed respect for libraries and librarians. Thanks to their collections I have been able to document my mother's eight-year modeling career via photographs from scores of magazines. I spent months visiting libraries across the country, scouring stacks of bound volumes containing fragile vintage magazines, their yellowed pages providing a window into another world. I would turn each page deliberately, and sit back when I stumbled on yet another image of my mother, knowing how an early prospector must have felt upon finding a nugget of gold. Special thanks to the Gladys Marcus Library at FIT, the Metropolitan Museum of Art Library, the New York Public Library, the Temple University Library, the Jefferson County Library Sciappa Branch (thank you to Sandy Day for sending so many articles from my mother's past), and the Library of Congress in Washington, D.C. (thank you to Cheryl Adams). And to all the magazine collectors on eBay! Thank you for respecting the past and not throwing out those old editions. My collection includes more than eighty magazines featuring my mother; they are treasures to me, and I would not have them otherwise.

Fred and Margarite Franitza, who bought the house on Long Island from my parents. Thank you for welcoming me into your home over the years. Revisiting the Dream House helped trigger many important memories from my youth.

Lloyd Harbor Elementary School. Thank you to Celia McGann for helping arrange my visit, and to Phil Gray, assistant principal, and Valerie Massimo, principal, for taking the time to speak with me. Thank you to Annette DiPietro for the school records. Your students are lucky to have such a devoted staff and beautiful environment in which to learn and grow. Visiting the school was incredibly helpful—it brought back some important memories and gave me some much-needed closure.

ACKNOWLEDGMENTS

Fay Krupski. I'm so thankful for your friendship during my childhood years. I'm equally grateful that I was able to speak with you during the process of writing this book.

The Cold Spring Harbor High School Reunion. It was wonderful to reconnect with friends from middle school, including Diana Stusvick, Gail Calumet, Kristin Hamlin, and Jeff Springsteen. Through Facebook I was able to connect with many of my sister Robin's friends, including Donna Wellman, Claudia Wellman, and Jean Williamson Carter.

My father's friends Roger Yussain, Ross Muerer, Diahn and Tom McGrath, and Jan Royal. Thank you for your valuable insights.

Chendo Perez. We met at a time when I desperately needed to be part of a family and have someone to love. Thank you for sharing your memories of my mother and of our time together while I was researching this book.

Skip Denenberg. You were such an important part of my sister Robin's life and like a brother to me all those years ago. It means the world to me that we have reconnected.

Ruthie Berman. Thank you for being such a good friend to Robin and for sharing your memories of her.

A special thank-you to Haven, Ted, Gil, and Wil Colgate for including me in their mother Marlene's eightieth birthday celebration on the same beach where we used to play as children. I am grateful that I was able to spend time with Marlene.

To the people who took care of my mother along the way, I wish I could personally thank each one of you from the bottom of my heart. There was a family of helpers out there, even if I didn't always know it at the time.

Thank you to social worker Susan Goodman, who worked with

my mother at the Park Avenue Armory, for deepening my understanding of my mother during her years there.

I am so grateful to the nurses at Medford Multicare, Brookhaven Hospital, and Sachem Adult Home for the loving care my mother received while she was there.

I thank the many women and mentors who filled the holes my mother left behind.

My dear friend Stephanie Schwartz. Thank you for listening to me daily as the story unfolded, encouraging me every step of the way, and for connecting me with so many important people. Shortly before Eve contacted me, I had made a very impassioned post on Facebook honoring Bill Barnes, a hero to me. (Bill is the executive director of the Clearview School, a school for emotionally disturbed children that my daughter attended for eleven years and where I had also served as vice president.) This post prompted you to call me and encouraged me to pursue my passion of mental health advocacy. You connected me with Audrey Brooks at the Mental Health Association of Westchester, an organization that has become an inspiration to me.

Audrey Brooks. In our first meeting, you asked if I had ever thought of writing a memoir, and later if my husband and I would chair the organization's 2015 Run/Walk in support of mental health advocacy, which we did. Thank you for your encouragement.

Doris Schwartz, former COO of the MHA of Westchester. You have served as a mentor to me in many ways. Your example and dedication have deepened my commitment to mental health advocacy. I am so grateful for the time you have given me.

Karen and Joel Berman. Thank you for helping me to obtain a copy of the 1993 *Hard Copy* episode featuring my mother. Thank you to CTD Clip Licensing Group for providing that episode so I could watch it again.

ACKNOWLEDGMENTS

Cathy Nish. Thank you for connecting us with Tony Monaco, the current manager of the Barbizon building on East Sixty-third Street. Tony, thank you for taking us on the tour of the former hotel. It was just wonderful to be inside the building, to walk out on its terraces, to learn of its history, and to stand on the floor near the rooms where Grace and my mother lived. It was especially valuable for us to have the original floor plan of the hotel.

I did not set out to focus on my mother's diagnosis, but this aspect became a very important part of the story. I am so grateful to have been able to share my mother's story with Dr. Jeffrey Lieberman, Dr. Diana Lynn Barnes, Dr. Dominic Grecco, and Ariane Sroubik. Your input was simply invaluable, adding to my understanding of my mother in ways I could have never predicted when I began my research. Thank you for the gift of your time and your expertise.

My therapist, Ginger Benlifer. Writing this book has been one of the most difficult things I have ever done, bringing on daily tears as I allowed myself to feel the sadness of my mother's life and to relive painful events that I had long suppressed. Toward the end of writing you helped me to talk through so many difficult memories. I don't think I could have gotten through it without your guidance.

Many authors have inspired me along the way—Andrew Solomon, Patrick Kennedy, and Regina Calcaterra. The honesty with which you shared your stories gave me the confidence to tell mine. I have seen the results of your work and the wonderful things that have come out of your desire to help others.

I have been incredibly lucky to be surrounded by my amazing modern family, whose endless love is both precious and strong.

My daughter Nicole. You are my angel who inspires me to deepen my conviction as an advocate.

My son, now known as Johnny Ferro. You chose to pursue your

dreams as an actor, and I'm so proud of all you have achieved. You have always shown great interest in my story, and have been an important sounding board throughout the entire journey. Thank you for building our website, too.

My daughter Danielle. Watching you graduate from college was easily one of the most important moments in my life—and to see you succeed in your career continues to bring me great joy as a proud mother.

My sisters, Robin and Jyl, and my half sister, Patricia Reybold. We shared a bond from birth. Patricia—thank you for making me feel connected, for our close relationship, and for the many wonderful memories we share.

David Weiss, thank you for being a wonderful father to our children, and for bringing Maya into our lives.

My stepdaughters, Kristin, Lauren, Jess, and her husband, Matt.

ACKNOWLEDGMENTS

Thank you for being such an important part of my life. Special thanks to Jess, the art director, for your help in bringing all the vintage images of my mother to life.

My amazing "Uncousins" family. The traditions we share have made up for much that was missing in my life.

My husband, Peter Giles. You always bring out the best in me, and you have encouraged me to shine even at the darkest moments. Without you, I never would have found the confidence to follow my dreams and share this story. You are my moral compass, my rock, my best friend—and an exceptional on-call editor when I needed a fresh eye for this book.

FROM EVE: Thank you to everyone above as well as my incredible team at Unfurl Productions; my ideal reader, Katie Simon; and my beloved family—Ros, John, Ruth, Hannah, Sacha, Zou Zou, Françoise, Philip, Zizi, Sam, Clara, Joe, and, above all, Chris, Grace, Rose, and Jack. Thank you, Nyna, for taking me on this journey with you, for sharing your life and your mother's story, and for being the kindest, most diligent collaborator imaginable. We got there in the end. . . .

MENTAL HEALTH RESOURCES

My mother's illness went untreated for so many years. Had she been diagnosed and properly treated, I believe her life and mine would have turned out very differently. For those who are facing mental health issues today—either of your own or within your families—I strongly encourage you to seek out the following organizations offering vital information and support.

American Psychiatric Association
www.psychiatry.org

Bring Change to Mind
www.bringchange2mind.org

Campaign to Change Direction
www.changedirection.org

Heads Together (UK)
www.headstogether.org.uk

Kennedy Forum

www.kennedyforum.org

Mental Health America

www.nmha.org

Mind (UK)

www.mind.org.uk

National Alliance on Mental Illness

www.nami.org

National Council for Behavioral Health

www.thenationalcouncil.org

National Institute of Mental Health (NIMH)

www.nimh.nih.gov

The following organizations offer information and support for women with postpartum health issues:

Postpartum Support International

www.postpartum.net

International Marcé Society for Perinatal Mental Health

www.marcesociety.com

Best Beginnings (UK)

www.bestbeginnings.org.uk

Anna Freud National Centre for Children and Families (UK)

www.annafreud.org

SOURCES

In order to tell the story of my mother's early years and her friendship with Grace, I had to rely on a number of sources, including the following:

Books and Articles on Grace Kelly

"The Girl in White Gloves." *Time,* 1955.

"Hollywood's Hottest Property." *Life,* April 26, 1954.

Kelly, Mrs. John B. "My Daughter Grace Kelly," nationally syndicated series of articles, 1956.

Lacey, Robert. *Grace.* New York: Putnam, 1994.

Leigh, Wendy. *True Grace: The Life and Times of an American Princess.* New York: St Martin's Press, 2007.

Quine, Judith Balaban. *The Bridesmaids: Grace Kelly, Princess of Monaco, and Six Intimate Friends.* New York: Weidenfeld and Nicholson, 1989.

Spoto, Donald. *High Society: The Life of Grace Kelly.* London: Hutchinson, 2009.

Other Sources

Beaton, Cecil. *Cecil Beaton: Memoirs of the '40s*. New York: McGraw-Hill, 1973.

Hasbrouck, Muriel Bruce. *The Pursuit of Destiny*. New York: E. P. Dutton, 1941.

Homans, Jennifer. *Apollo's Angels: A History of Ballet*. New York: Random House, 2010.

Lacey, Robert. *Model Woman: Eileen Ford and the Business of Beauty*. New York: Harper, 2015.

Stewart-Gordon, Faith. *The Russian Tea Room: A Love Story*. New York: Scribner, 1999.

Articles on the Barbizon Hotel for Women in *Collier's* (1948), *Saturday Evening Post* (1953), *Philadelphia Daily News* (1982), *Vanity Fair* (2010).

Articles about contemporary models from *Kansas City Star* (1946), *Harrisburg Telegraph* (1945), *Abilene Reporter-News* (1948).

Articles on the Ford Modeling Agency in *Life* (1948) and *Photography Workshop* (1950).

Articles about my mother in *Star* (1989), *Hello* (1989), and *New York Post* (1993), and a clipping from a local Ohio newspaper (name unknown) about my mother's career from 1951.

TV segments about my mother on *Current Affair* (1989) and *Hard Copy* (1993).

Landmarks Preservation Commission reports on the Barbizon and Manhattan House buildings.

In addition, I was able to draw on family photographs, my mother's modeling photos, her medical records, the few letters I have from her, my school records, my sister Robin's school records, and Robin's notes about our time in France and the period after we returned, newspaper articles about Robin during the period of her "welfare scandal," and interviews with my mother's family members and friends.

PHOTOGRAPH CREDITS

Page 8: Carolyn Schaffner in striped skirt, 1947 (Charles F. Green—Jefferson County Historical Association)

Page 11: Carolyn as Sesquicentennial Queen, 1947 (Charles F. Green—Jefferson County Historical Association)

Page 26: Carolyn yearbook photo, 1946

Page 26: Grace Kelly yearbook photo, 1947

Page 31: Carolyn in J'ray ad (on right), *Mademoiselle* magazine, May, 1948

Page 34: Nina Reybold, Long Island, 1964 (Author's Private Collection)

Page 45: Carolyn Schaffner in Gorham Sterling Silver ad, June 1948 (Gorham Division of Lenox Corporation)

Page 48: Ford Models by Nina Leen, 1948 (Nina Leen/The LIFE Picture Collection/Getty Images)

Page 49: Carolyn Scott, *McCall's* magazine, August 1948 (Meredith Corporation, Photograph by Richard Avedon, © The Richard Avedon Foundation)

Page 53: Carolyn, *Seventeen* magazine, November 1948 (The Francesco Scavullo Foundation, © The Francesco Scavullo Trust)

Page 64: Grace Kelly modeling at age nineteen, 1949 (Alamy Inc.)

Page 64: Carolyn, *Charm* magazine, June 1949 (© Gleb Derujinsky)

Page 69: Carolyn and Malcolm Reybold at the Stork Club (Photo courtesy of Stork Club Enterprises LLC, all rights reserved)

Page 72: Carolyn, Sears Catalogue, 1949 (Sears Corporate)

Page 82: Carolyn and Malcolm Reybold cutting their wedding cake, March 1949 (Author's Private Collection)

Page 87: Carolyn, Long Island (Author's Private Collection)

Page 90: Carolyn, *Mademoiselle* magazine, February 1951 (© George Barkentin)

Page 98: Carolyn with daughters, Jill and Robin, Manhattan House, 1953 (Author's Private Collection)

Page 119: Grace Kelly, Oleg Cassini, Carolyn Reybold (© Bettmann/Getty Images)

Page 126: Sally Richardson and Carolyn Reybold (© Bettmann/Getty Images)

Page 131: Princess Grace of Monaco in her wedding dress. Hercule's Gallery, Palace of Monaco, April 19, 1956 (Photo by Fernand Detaille, © Archives du Palais de Monaco)

Page 133: Royal Wedding bridesmaids 1956 (Joseph Mckeown Hulton Royals Collection/Getty Images)

Page 135: Grace visiting shrine, April 1956 (Haywood Magee Hulton Royals Collection/Getty Images)

Page 144: Robin Reybold in Cannes, France, April 1972 (Author's Private Collection)

Page 152: Dream House, Long Island (Author's Private Collection)

Page 176: Carolyn and baby Nina, February 1960 (Author's Private Collection)

Page 181: Carolyn with her three daughters, summer 1960 (Author's Private Collection)

Page 189: Nyna wearing bridesmaid's dress (Douglas Wright, Author's Private Collection

PHOTOGRAPH CREDITS

Page 200: Carolyn all in white, NYC 1989 (© Paul Adao)

Page 206: Nyna's children: Michael, Danielle, and Nicole, 1995 (Author's Private Collection)

Page 210: Carolyn and Nyna at Medford Multicare, Long Island (Author's Private Collection)

Page 244: Carolyn's favorite headshot (Author's Private Collection)

Page 256: Nyna's family at her stepdaughter Jessica's wedding, February 2015; *left to right*: Danielle, Kristin, Nyna, Matt, Jessica, Peter, Lauren, and Johnny (Photo by Christina Szczupak)

Page 266: Robin Reybold (Author's Private Collection)

In Memory of Robin Reybold, 1953–1979